GROWING IN THE PROPHETIC

'Mike Bickle is a man with a remarkable teaching gift, quick to acknowledge past mistakes which he has clearly learned from. This is a book every charismatic should read if we are going to increase our ability to hear from God, speak to him, and remain committed to Christ, to Scripture and to one another.'

Gerald Coates, Pioneer

'Mike Bickle's thoroughly scriptural and Christ-centred teaching and message provide the ideal background for assessing the current move of prophecy within the church. This book is a milestone in the recovery of God's church in the end times and I would recommend Mike and the message to all who are serious about moving on with God.'

Roger Forster, Ichthus Fellowship

Growing in the Prophetic

MIKE BICKLE
WITH **MICHAEL SULLIVANT**

KINGSWAY PUBLICATIONS
EASTBOURNE

ISBN 0 85476 554 9

Produced by Bookprint Creative Services
P.O. Box 827, BN21 3YJ, England, for
KINGSWAY PUBLICATIONS LTD
Lottbridge Drove, Eastbourne, E Sussex BN23 6NT.
Printed in Great Britain.

I want first to dedicate this book to the faithful congregation of Metro Vineyard Fellowship, who courageously stuck by me for the last twelve years as we continued on the journey to be a prophetic church. They have seen God's glory on several occasions and yet endured many perils because I had neither the maturity nor the wisdom to pastor prophetic people in a proper way. I thank you, Metro Vineyard Fellowship.

Also, I want to dedicate this book to Paul Cain whose fatherly love and wisdom have made a great difference in my life. Paul's exceptional prophetic gifts have astounded me on many occasions. His mature wisdom has led me out of confusion and perplexity time and time again. His godly example of meekness and kindness has challenged me to follow him as he follows Christ. Last, but not least, his fatherly love has given me the security and courage not to give up. Thank you, Paul.

Acknowledgements

I want to express my deep appreciation to Walter Walker who initially came up with the idea for this book. He relentlessly pursued me to meet deadlines and actually to complete the book. He interviewed Michael Sullivant and myself for many hours, then took the transcriptions and turned them into the pages of this book. God has greatly blessed me with a truly skilled and yet humble ghost-writer. Thank you, Walter, for your abilities and your great heart.

Also, I want to thank Jane Joseph for the endless hours of overtime that she has dedicated to this book. A prophetic secretary is as valuable as a prophetic ghost-writer. She too is a gift of God.

Last, but not least, I want to thank my precious wife, Diane, and my two wonderful sons, Luke and Paul, for allowing me to sacrifice some of our time together to write this book.

Contents

Foreword

1. There's Been a Terrible Mistake   11
2. The Coming Great Visitation   25
3. Confirming Prophecies Through the
   Acts of God in Nature   35
4. False Equations About Spiritual Giftings   57
5. God Offends the Mind to Reveal the Heart   75
6. Embodying the Prophetic Message   91
7. Stoning False Prophets   107
8. God's Strategy of Silence   121
9. Origins of the Prophetic Call   133
10. Pastors and Prophets: Getting Along in the Kingdom   153
11. The Prophetic Word in Public Worship   169
12. The Prophetic Song of the Lord   183
13. Revelation, Interpretation and Application   193
14. Women as Prophetic Ministers   205
15. Eight Dimensions of the Prophetic Church   215

Appendix I: 'God's Manifest Presence'   227
Appendix II: MVF's Mission Statement   239
Appendix III: Grace Training Center   243
Appendix IV: Mike Bickle's teaching tapes, books,
   conferences   249

Foreword

Mike Bickle has had the unusual – possibly unique – experience of leading a large church which has been built up since its very beginning through prophecies from various people. He understands the blessing of the prophetic gift and spells out many useful lessons he has had to learn, sometimes by painful experience, including a number of false charges which were compiled and widely distributed by a now discredited leader of a large church in Kansas City.

So often in the past prophecy has fallen into disrepute. This was partly due to the mistakes of those giving the prophecies, and partly to the hostility of traditional church leaders, who can feel threatened by it, are ignorant about how to handle it, and who have tried almost successfuly to quench it. But it is clearly an important gift of the Holy Spirit imparted to the New Testament Christians and becoming increasingly manifested once again in today's church – especially following the recent move of the Holy Spirit. Mike's conviction that prophecy is for today, and the positive lessons he has learned as a church leader handling prophetic capability in the congregation, are singularly helpful.

Mike reveals a deep knowledge of the human heart, and his

insights are certainly relevant to the understanding of prophetically gifted people. He shares his own passion for Jesus, which is the spirit of prophecy. He also shares his sense of bewilderment in his early confrontations with some prophetic people.

This book is timely. It is written with a light touch and profound insight. As one committed to the creation of a pool of wisdom for coping with prophecy in the local church, I welcome this most wholesome contribution to the subject.

David Pytches
May 1995

1

There's Been a Terrible Mistake

John Wimber had set it all up. It was July 1989, and 4,000 people crowded into a warehouse converted into a church building that was being used by the Vineyard Christian Fellowship in Anaheim, California.

John had spoken a couple of times at the conference, then introduced Paul Cain, myself and others who were going to bring messages on the prophetic ministry. I taught on the nurturing and administration of the prophetic ministry in the local church, and offered some practical advice to encourage laymen with prophetic giftings. These two ideas are the main topics of this book. I also related some stories about how we had periodically seen God use dreams, visions, angels and his audible voice to accomplish his purposes in our church life. I even shared a few stories about God confirming some of these prophetic revelations with signs in nature—for example, comets, earthquakes, droughts and floods occurring at precisely predicted times.

I guess I should have been more clear about the fact that very seldom do any of these supernatural experiences ever happen through me. For the past twelve years I have been mostly a spectator of the prophetic ministry and, initially, a reluctant one at that. In my early days of ministry, I was a young, conservative evangelical pastor hoping one day to attend Dallas Theological Seminary. I was very anti-charismatic and proud of it. Within a few short years, I found myself surrounded by and caught up with a small group of unusual people whom some referred to as prophets. 'Why me, Lord?' I asked many times.

Paul Cain is a grand old saint and a dear friend whose prophetic ministry is nothing short of astounding. His ministry earlier in that conference, along with my prophetic stories, must have overloaded some people's spiritual circuit-breakers. These were predominantly conservative evangelical church people who had been blessed by Wimber's theology on healing, but for the most part had not been exposed to any kind of prophetic ministry. There is, I have discovered, a great longing throughout the body of Christ. People are desperate to hear from God in a personal way.

I finished my session, and we were about to break for lunch. At the last minute John Wimber came up onto the platform and whispered in my ear, 'Would you pray and ask the Holy Spirit to release the gift of prophecy to people?'

If you've been around John Wimber at all, you'll know that there's not an ounce of hype or showmanship in him. He'll invite the Holy Spirit to move over an audience to touch thousands of people with the same tone of voice he'll use to give the last announcement. It was in that matter-of-fact way that he asked me to pray for the people to receive what I had just been describing.

With 4,000 spiritually hungry people watching us, I whispered back to John, 'Can I do that, since I'm not prophetically gifted myself?'

John responded, 'Just go ahead and pray for the release and let the Lord touch whomever he will.'

Why am I praying for these people? I thought. I started looking around for help from Paul Cain, John Paul Jackson or someone who might know what they were doing. But I was obviously on my own. It would be a harmless prayer, I supposed. *Well OK, John. If you want me to*, I thought.

So John announced that I was going to ask the Holy Spirit to release the gift of prophecy in people's lives. I had just introduced Paul Cain, Bob Jones and the others—men who had for years operated in prophetic ministry in a way that had amazed me. It seems, however, that some of the people had mistakenly determined that I was an anointed prophet and certainly the man to see if they wanted the prophetic gift released in them. Bob Scott, my brother-in-law, who helped me start the church, was at the back of the room quietly laughing to himself. He knew I was not a prophet, and he also knew that I was in deep waters, way over my head.

As soon as the meeting was over a long line of people waited anxiously to talk to me. Some wanted me to pray personally for the prophetic gift to be imparted to them. Others wanted me to give them a 'word from the Lord', that is, to prophesy what God wanted to say about them and his plan for their lives. Over and over again I explained, 'No, I don't have a word for you. No, I can't impart prophetic gifts. No, I'm not prophetically gifted.'

I looked around for John, but could not find him. After spending some time explaining this one by one to about twenty-five people who were standing in line, I simply stood up on the stage and made a loud announcement: 'There's been a terrible mistake! I don't have a prophetic ministry!'

The previous day John Wimber had introduced me to Richard Foster, author of *Celebration of Discipline*. Richard had been waiting for me to finish praying for people so that we could go to lunch. I was starving and wanted us to get as far away as we could as fast as we could.

Heading for the car, I was stopped by several people in the car park who also wanted me to prophesy to them. Of course, I had no prophetic words for them.

Finally we made our escape and found a restaurant about ten miles from the meeting place. But to my surprise, while I was standing at the salad bar with a plate of food in my hand, I was asked by two different people who had attended the conference to prophesy to them. Then a couple came over to our table, wondering if I had a prophetic word for them. I now wished that I had made it more clear during my session that I was not a prophet nor the son of a prophet. Actually, I am the son of a professional boxer.

For many people, all that they know about God is in the context of things far away and long ago. They are hungry to know that God is involved with their lives in an intimate way in the present tense. When that knowledge is dramatically awakened for the first time, people—myself include—often overreact for a short season.

All of this was overwhelming to me. Those who are either excited or desperate to hear from God are seldom restrained and polite. I was getting impatient and exasperated with people's persistence. The fact that I was with Richard Foster, whom I had wanted to meet for a long time, increased my irritation. It was really very embarrassing. You'd never guess by reading *Celebration of Discipline* that the author is a spontaneous comedian. He roared with laughter when I laid my plate down and said to him, 'Richard, I'm not a prophetic person! A terrible mistake has been made today.'

That situation was insignificant compared to the uproar that was to come a few years later. It was neither the first time nor the last time I felt that God had picked the wrong person to pastor a team of prophetic people.

A reluctant introduction to prophetic ministry

Our experience has been that many people, both leaders and laymen, who have involved themselves with ministries that embrace the prophetic, have been brought in kicking and screaming. My close friend, Dr Jack Deere, was formerly a professor at Dallas Theological Seminary and a committed cessationist[1] before he met John Wimber and experienced the demonstrations of God's power. He also went through a difficult, soul-searching journey as he came to embrace the prophetic ministry. With the attention we have received over the last few years with regard to people with prophetic giftings in our church, some are amazed to discover the type of people the Lord has brought to work with us. Eight of the men on our staff have master's degrees, plus another four of them have earned doctorates—all from conservative evangelical, non-charismatic seminaries. These men are in strong contrast to the prophetic ministers.

This contrast is great, but the diversity is essential. However, there are many tensions created by such different personalities. In fact, the Lord has helped us to establish a fairly academically challenging full-time Bible school called the Grace Training Center of Kansas City. The scholarly types and the prophetic ministers teach side by side as one ministry team that has learned to work in unity. We want to combine the gifts of the Spirit with a responsible scholarship in the Scriptures. Our Bible school has only been going for five years, but our students have given us encouraging reviews regarding the spiritual and biblical training that they have received. Like most people in our church, the majority of these seminary educated staff members of the Metro Vineyard leadership team are not highly prophetic. They are pastors and teachers who have felt a strong calling to be a part of a ministry that embraces, among other things, the prophetic ministry. The same is true for the majority

---

[1] One who believes that the supernatural gifts of the Holy Spirit manifested in the first century have now ceased.

of laymen in our church who have prophetic giftings. Their involvement in this type of ministry is often a contradiction to their early training against the spiritual gifts. So many times God's calling cuts directly across the grain of our natural strengths and previous doctrinal training. We believe that God wants to deeply integrate strong evangelical training in the Scriptures with supernatural manifestations of the Holy Spirit. This is one of the main reasons that we started Grace Training Center. I highly recommend Jack Deere's book, *Surprised by the Power of the Spirit* for those wanting more teaching on this subject.

Paul said in his letter to the Corinthians that God's strength was made perfect in his weakness (2 Cor 12:9). It is common for God to call people to something for which they are not naturally equipped. Peter, the uneducated fisherman, is called as an apostle to the educated Jews. Paul, the self-righteous Pharisee, is called as an apostle to the pagan Gentiles. To be called in weakness to do something needing great strength is similar to being called as a theological sceptic to be part of something supernatural. I certainly fit into that category, as do some of the people on the Metro Vineyard staff and many people in our church. No one would have ever suspected from our early religious training and affiliations that we would have been remotely involved in a prophetic ministry. God *must* have a sense of humour.

Another terrible mistake

In February 1972, at the age of sixteen, I was touched by the Holy Spirit's power. At an Assembly of God church in Kansas City named Evangel Temple the Holy Spirit seemed to engulf me, and I spoke in tongues for the first time. Before that experience, I had never even heard of the gift of tongues. I had no idea what had happened to me. I asked the people who prayed for me to help me understand what had happened. They said I had spoken in tongues. I asked, 'What is that?' They said I could learn more about it at the next meeting.

Though it was a powerful encounter with God, I was immediately convinced by my Presbyterian leaders that the experience was a demonic counterfeit. I eventually concluded that I had been deceived by this counterfeit experience. I fully renounced the experience and committed myself to resisting anything charismatic, because anything seeming so real could easily deceive other people. I set out to warn other 'innocent' believers to beware of such counterfeit experiences as speaking in tongues, and for the next several years it became my personal mission to debunk charismatic theology and rescue from deception anyone who had been led astray by such a 'counterfeit experience'.

I didn't like charismatic people any more than I liked charismatic theology. The ones I had met seemed to boast of having it all. I felt they were proud and arrogant. In my estimation, they were lacking in many things, especially passion for the Scriptures and personal holiness. Besides, their theology was not evangelically orthodox. As a young Christian I committed myself to being a student of evangelical greats, absorbing myself in the writings of J. I. Packer, John Stott, Stuart Briscoe, Jonathan Edwards, Dr Martyn Lloyd-Jones and others.

I took my zeal for evangelical orthodoxy and my crusade against supernatural gifts of the Spirit with me everywhere I ministered God's word. I spoke at a number of college campus ministries through the Midwest.

In April 1976 I was invited to give a trial sermon for a little Lutheran house church of twenty-five people who were searching for a pastor. They were interested in the renewal going on in the Lutheran Church. I preached an anti-charismatic version of the baptism of the Holy Spirit, a favourite sermon which I preached many times on college campuses. I took it straight from John Stott's little book on the baptism of the Holy Spirit. I wanted to make it clear from the beginning that I didn't want anything to do with charismatic heresies.

Although these people seemed to love the Lord greatly, they were not aware of all the various theological arguments against tongues and other gifts. They were interested in my becoming their pastor, and the doctrinal implications of my sermon went right over their heads. At the same time I was unaware that most of them were enjoying the Lutheran renewal movement. Their reserved demeanour fooled me. Some of the leading people of the prayer group were away that weekend. When they got back they heard that the young preacher had preached on the baptism of the Spirit. Well, that was good enough for them, and I was taken on. Those leading people who were away during my sermon assumed I was in agreement with their charismatic theology and I assumed they had been given an accurate report on my sermon that was filled with anti-charismatic theology. I was totally unsuspecting of what would happen next.

It was about six months later, and about seventy-five people were now attending the new church plant. One of the leaders who had been away during my original baptism in the Spirit sermon, pointed out to me that some of the newcomers had not yet received the baptism of the Spirit. He wanted me to extend the invitation and pray for them.

'But I do that every Sunday morning at the altar call for salvation.'

'No, no,' he said. 'We want the tongues part.'

'I don't believe in tongues,' I answered. It wasn't long before I realised what had happened. It then became clear for the first time that they had totally misunderstood my early arguments against charismatic doctrines. I groaned, 'Oh, there's been a terrible mistake!'

A part of me wanted to run away as fast as I could. I grimaced to myself. I was the *pastor* of a charismatic church! I couldn't believe it. How could I have landed myself in this mess? In retrospect, there was no doubt that it was God himself who had got me into it. By now I really liked these people and trusted their genuineness, their humility, their love for the Scriptures and for evangelism. How could such good people be charismatics? My experience with this church was God's way of breaking down some of my prejudices against charismatics. I now had a category of people I respected and accepted as authentic Christians, but who, in my mind, happened to be a little 'off' theologically. Mike Bickle was now tolerating charismatics. That was OK for now since I had made plans to go to Mexico as a missionary. I thought to myself, 'I could endure anything for a short season.'

I continued on for a few more months with the church before I encountered the first prophetic word aimed at me. It is amazing how we all got on with each other. I didn't believe in prophetic words or any of that bizarre stuff. One evening I went to hear the president of the Full Gospel Businessmen's Fellowship speak at a meeting. I was with some of the men from our church. The man called me out and said, 'Young man at the back. God's going to shift you from where you are, and you are going to stand before hundreds of young people—immediately.'

Not me, I thought to myself. I had already made the arrangements to work with a missionary organisation in Mexico. I thought I was saying goodbye to Western Christianity and going where the harvest was in Latin America. I had set my heart on spending my life in Mexico and South America. I was upset by this prophetic word and told myself that it could not be right.

Then the man said, 'Even though you say in your heart this very moment, "This cannot be," God will do it immediately.'

People were hugging me and clapping, but I was angry and just wanted to get out of there.

The very next week I was in St Louis with a friend and acci-
dentally met the pastor of a large charismatic church there. He
looked at me and said, 'I know we are strangers, but I have an
unusual request for you. The Spirit of God just spoke to me and
said that you're the one who is supposed to preach to our youth
service where over a thousand young people gather every Saturday night.'

Before I could think about it, I heard myself say, 'Yes.' I was
so shocked and confused in my own heart that I had spontaneously agreed to preach in this radical charismatic church. I
was embarrassed at myself. What would my friends think?

The Saturday night meeting went pretty well. At the end, the
pastor stood up in front of 1,000 applauding young people and
asked if I would come back the following week. Under the
pressure of the moment, I agreed to be the speaker the next
week, and the same thing happened on the following Saturday.
I found myself agreeing to come several more times. They were
so receptive to me that I thought I could change their theology.

The next month, on my wedding day, my elders had a private
meeting with this pastor during the wedding reception and
agreed that I should be the next youth pastor at this large charismatic church. Without ever consulting me, they simply made
this announcement at the end of the wedding reception. I was
so excited to be married to my wonderful wife, Diane, that I
simply responded, 'Great, I'll do anything you want!'

During my honeymoon, I couldn't believe how easily I had
agreed to leave my new little church to be a youth pastor at a
charismatic church. I asked myself, 'How could I let this happen?' It seemed I was constantly being ambushed by God to do
things I had prejudices against. I felt a desperate need to
reassert control over my life. I was now, of all things, on the
pastoral staff of New Covenant Fellowship, a radical charismatic church in St Louis, Missouri. How much worse could
things get?

I shared an office with an ex-Lutheran pastor named Tim Gustafson, who helped me to adjust to this strange new charismatic environment. Little did I realise that my reluctant journey into the gifts of the Spirit had just begun. I was still unsettled about the gift of tongues. The prophecy that I had received at the Full Gospel Businessmen's Fellowship meeting saying that I would immediately stand in front of hundreds of young people was fulfilled within two months. It was obviously fulfilled by my becoming the youth pastor of this large church in St Louis. However, I still didn't even believe in prophecy, so I could never have imagined what would happen in the years ahead. I chose to ignore the fact that this prophecy had been realised. I thought it was a coincidence. I still had plans to go to Mexico, so I would simply be patient with this charismatic church, just like I had been with the last one.

But I was a conservative Evangelical who was about to get involved with spiritual gifts, particularly the gift of prophecy, on a level that seemed very unusual, even to many charismatics.

In the spring of 1979, that church leadership asked me to consider turning over the youth ministry to start a new sister church that would relate to them. So in September 1979, I became the pastor of a new church plant in South St Louis County. The church was growing, and Diane and I assumed that we would serve there for many years. I was beginning to give up the idea of being a missionary to Mexico. That God would have a different plan for us wasn't so strange, but the way he communicated his plan to us presented another great challenge to our faith.

Now it was June 1982, three years after this new church was founded, I was confronted by people, including Bob Jones, who claimed to have had divine encounters with God. These unusual experiences they talked about included audible voices, angelic visitations, Technicolor visions and signs in the heavens, to name a few of the more spectacular ones. Some of these divine communiqués seemed to have major implications for the direction of my life and ministry. I wondered, if God was so interested in getting my attention, why didn't he just give me my own vision, despite the fact that I didn't have much faith in the validity of such experiences? I had fully accepted the idea of God healing the sick, but I wasn't prepared for the idea of such prophetic experiences.

At first their claims seemed to me to be the stuff of vivid but misguided imaginations and not a genuine revelation from God. But as I listened and prayed, the Holy Spirit began to confirm their genuineness. At the same time, my most trusted friends and co-workers also began believing these were true prophecies. Though all of this ran contrary to some long-term reservations about this kind of thing, I decided to take a step of faith and allow for the prophetic ministry in our church. I could never have understood the remarkable things that God would do in our church or in my personal life, nor did I foresee the trouble it would get me into.

The Lord used prophetic words confirmed in some extraordinary ways to relocate us from St Louis to the Kansas City area. There we began another church plant in December 1982. In 1990, we affiliated with the Association of Vineyard Churches and are now known as Metro Vineyard Fellowship. Since 1983, our leadership team has discovered that prophetic ministry can bring great blessing to the church. We have also come to realise that it can cause confusion, condemnation and can be counterproductive to God's purposes if not administrated properly. In our early days, David Parker, currently an excellent pastor of a large Vineyard church in Lancaster, California, was on our staff and he helped our church immensely by putting a sound theological framework around the prophetic ministry. He has a mature ability to embrace the ministry of the Holy Spirit in a context of responsible biblical scholarship.

A few people with prophetic ministries who ministered among us in the first couple of years of this new church no longer do so. There were various reasons for their departure. Some of these were painful but necessary confrontations that our fellowship weathered and from which we have emerged wiser and more seasoned. Through this book we hope to share insights we have painfully but joyfully gathered. It's been a very unusual journey. I could never have imagined the dramatic unfolding of events that was to take place.

2

The Coming Great Visitation

I am thankful that God never intended the prophetic ministry at
our church in Kansas City to become a 'prophetic movement'.
It was referred to in that manner by people who later became
opponents and critics. We saw ourselves as simply a church-
planting team that contained some prophetic ministers, just as it
contained pastors, teachers, evangelists and administrators. In
my mind, the predominant feature was to be passion for Jesus
and intercession for revival. Nevertheless, the prophetic people
who ended up ministering among us seemed so extraordinary
that their contributions became the notable feature, especially
to those who viewed us from the outside. The events associated
with the prophetic seemed so unusual and intriguing that the
message of holy passion, intercession and revival was sometimes overshadowed. Thus it was negatively tagged a prophetic
movement, and we were called 'the Kansas City prophets'.
Inside our local church the prophetic also gained too high a pro-
file, but still it was not the primary emphasis of what our leadership team was aiming to accomplish. I was continually seeking to keep our church focused on one of our primary
purposes—interceding for the great revival I believe is still to
come. A revival that would see countless multitudes of new

believers coming into the church. A revival that would see the church restored to the passion, purity, power and unity of the New Testament.

Prophecy is not something on which a church should major. It is one of the many tools used to build the house, but it's not the house. When you construct a building you don't call a hammer a movement. The hammer is just one of the many significant tools.

We first moved to Kansas City in November 1982 to start the church. Several weeks before we had our first Sunday service, we began nightly intercessory prayer meetings. We had about fifteen people, and we met from 7.00 to 10.00 every single night, seven days a week. These continued every night for ten years with few exceptions for holidays like Thanksgiving and Christmas.

In October 1984, when our church was almost two years old, we added two more daily intercessory prayer meetings. We met three times each day: 6.30–8.30am, 11.30–1.00pm and 7.00–10.00pm. For six hours a day we mobilised our church to intercede, first for revival in Kansas City and America and then the Lord spoke to us to pray for key places like England, Germany and Israel. Most of these intercessory prayer meetings had between twenty and fifty people in attendance. From 1987 to 1989, we multiplied into six different congregations throughout the city. We sought to function as one church structure, yet meeting in six places. Each congregation would then take some of the responsibility for these daily prayer meetings. In 1992, we released three of those congregations to operate as independent churches. The other two merged back into the central worship centre. Today at Metro Vineyard Fellowship we still have intercessory prayer meetings three times a day on Mondays, Wednesdays and Fridays.

In all, for the last twelve years we have been pretty heavily committed to intercession for a coming great visitation of God.

I say all this because intercession is one of the primary purposes of the prophetic ministry in Kansas City. Regrettably, we
did a poor job at pastoring our people and evangelising our
community. Today our church is based on small fellowship
groups. We encourage everyone to participate in these home
groups and to be involved in our regular servant evangelism
projects. Consequently, we cannot maintain the same level of
commitment to intercession that we did during the first ten
years of our church's history. Things are more balanced
between pastoral care and evangelism, yet we need to be continually inspired by the prophetic ministry so as to maintain the
intercessory prayer meetings three times a day for three days a
week.

In the past, to people who were viewing our ministry from
the outside, the prophetic ministries were powerful and intriguing. Consequently, it took on a certain notoriety, and our church
became identified with the prophetic ministry. But to us
prophetic ministry, with its astounding features, and prophecies
confirmed by things like comets, droughts and earthquakes,
were mostly aimed at one thing: encouraging and sustaining
our intercession for revival of the church. God wants the church
to experience a great harvest of new souls who come to maturity in the grace of God and specifically in their passionate
affection for Jesus.

Prophecy should never be an end in itself. It was because of
the prophecies that we were encouraged to stay faithful to the
daily prayer meetings and to focus on a life of loving passion
for Jesus. I believe prophetic ministry is the fuel that runs the
tanks of intercession and purity. It is the prophetic hope that
causes our prayers for a coming great visitation of God to be
persistent through the many years and the diverse seasons of
hardship.

Exegesis and prophetic revelation

For us, the whole concept of nurturing and administrating the prophetic ministry in the local church is an outgrowth of our expectation of an outpouring of the Holy Spirit as foretold in Joel 2 and cited by Peter's first sermon on the Day of Pentecost. 'And it shall come to pass in the last days, says God, that I will pour out of My Spirit on all flesh' (Acts 2:17).

For years I had read Jonathan Edwards, David Brainerd, Martyn Lloyd-Jones and some of the Puritan writers, and had adopted their theology of an unprecedented ingathering of souls at the end of the age. (I highly recommend Iain Murray's book called *The Puritan Hope*.) But it was years later in a dirty little motel room in Cairo, Egypt, when the belief in a last-days outpouring of the Holy Spirit became a personal issue. At that time I wholly committed my life to be a part of it. Concerning a last-days outpouring of the Holy Spirit, the scriptural basis and historical precedents must always come before prophetic revelation and personal experience that is subjective. The strongest kind of faith comes from when you both *understand* it based on the Scriptures and *discern* it by the Spirit.

One characteristic of many Old Testament prophecies about God's kingdom is that the prophetic fulfilments are sometimes manifested in two ways. First, there was a local fulfilment in Israel in the first coming of Christ, the outpouring of the Spirit at Pentecost and the birth of the church. Secondly, the complete fulfilment of revival will only be manifested with a worldwide scope just before the Second Coming of Christ.

Nevertheless, Jesus spoke of the kingdom not only as if the kingdom had come, but also as if it was still yet to come. As George E. Ladd puts it, the kingdom was both already and not yet. The kingdom has come with the advent of Christ, but the complete manifestation of prophecies concerning the kingdom of God will occur at the end of the age when Jesus Christ returns again.

In the last two verses of the Old Testament, Malachi had prophesied: 'Behold, I will send you Elijah the prophet before the coming of the great and dreadful day of the Lord' (Mal 4:5). Jesus identified John as Elijah (Mt 11:14) and later said of him, 'Elijah is coming first and will restore all things. But I say to you that Elijah has come already, and they did not know him but did to him whatever they wished' (Mt 17:11–12). We see an immediate local fulfilment of 'Elijah's' coming in John the Baptist's ministry in Judea. However, we also see a future fulfilment when 'Elijah' will come to restore all things at the end of the age.

In the same way, the Joel 2 prophecies concerning the outpouring of the Holy Spirit are partially fulfilled in Jerusalem at the Day of Pentecost. Peter quotes the prophecies and says, 'These are not drunk, as you suppose, since it is only the third hour of the day. But this is what was spoken by the prophet Joel' (Acts 2:15–16).

Because the outpouring at Pentecost was 'that which was spoken through the prophet Joel' doesn't mean this was *all* of that. The Spirit fell on 120 people in a room in Jerusalem. That's not big enough for the complete fulfilment, even if you include the 3,000 who were converted and baptised that day. The prophecy of Joel says, 'I will pour out My Spirit on *all flesh*' (Joel 2:28).

I am convinced that the fullness of Joel 2 is yet to be seen. It will have a worldwide scope to it, where all flesh—that is all believers, not just prophets—will have dreams and see visions. The greatest and fullest manifestation of the kingdom of God, the Day of the Lord, the restoration of all things and the outpouring of the Holy Spirit are reserved for the consummation of all things at the end of the age. I believe there will be an unprecedented revival, complete with all believers experiencing dreams and visions, just before the Second Coming of Christ.

Changing the face of Christianity in one generation

By September 1982 I had resigned from South County Christian Fellowship in St Louis after planting that church three years earlier with my dear friend Harry Schroeder. We had not planned to arrive in Kansas City until early November, so I accepted an invitation to speak at a pastors' conference in India. Since I had one of those thirty-day, go-anywhere-you-want tickets, I spent another two weeks visiting five major third-world cities. I wanted to use this opportunity to see the 'poor of the earth'. I went to the slum areas of each of these major cities.

I arrived in Cairo, Egypt, in mid-September. Following the suggestions of a taxi driver, I checked into a little hotel. The 8 × 8 room was equipped with a small bed, squeaky ceiling fan, stone-age plumbing and an assortment of crawling things that periodically scampered across the concrete floor. It was primitive by Western standards.

I was spending time every day interceding for my future church plant in Kansas City. That was a continual burden on my heart. I began to pray at around 8.30 that evening. I had been kneeling on the cement floor by the rickety bed for about thirty minutes when I had one of the most incredible encounters that I have ever had. I didn't see a vision, and I wasn't caught up into heaven. I simply heard God speak to me. It wasn't what some people call the audible voice. I call it the internal audible voice. I heard it as clearly as I would have heard it with my physical ears and, honestly, it was terrifying. It was such a feeling of cleanness, power and authority. In some ways I felt I was being crushed by it. I wanted to leave, but I didn't want to leave. I wanted it to be over, but I didn't want it to be over.

There were only a few sentences, and it took just a few moments, but every word had great meaning. The awe of God flooded my soul as I experienced a little bit of the terror of the

Lord. I literally trembled and wept as God himself was communicating to me in a way I've never known before or since. The Lord simply said, 'I will change the understanding and expression of Christianity in the earth in one generation.' It's a simple, straightforward statement, but I felt God's power with each word as I received the Spirit's interpretation.

I understood that this reformation/revival would be his sovereign initiative. It is God himself who is going to make this drastic change of Christianity across the world. The phrase 'the understanding of Christianity' means the way Christianity is perceived by unbelievers. In the early church people were afraid to associate even casually with believers, partly because of the displays of supernatural power. In the 1990s most unbelievers consider the church to be irrelevant. God will change the way unbelievers view the church. Once again they will witness God's wonderful yet terrifying power in the church. They will have a very different understanding of Christianity before God is finished with this generation.

The phrase 'expression of Christianity' means the way the body of Christ expresses its life together. I believe God is going to change this powerfully so that the church functions as a healthy body in the power and love of God, instead of just being meeting- and programme-based in its design and structure.

Paul Cain says that there are three elements of this new understanding and expression: unparalleled power, purity and unity. Christians' relationship with God and with each other, the way they are perceived by unbelievers and even the structure and functioning of the church are going to be radically and swiftly changed by God himself. And this change will take place, not in a month, a year or a few years, but in one generation. I had the sense that I was being invited to be part of this.

The understanding and expression of Christianity is going to be changed by a great outpouring of the Spirit that will cross all kinds of national, social, ethnic and cultural barriers. It won't just be a Western world revival. The Joel 2/Acts 2 prophecy says that in the last days God will pour out his Spirit on 'all flesh' (Acts 2:17).

A lot of things will begin to happen as a result of this out-pouring of the Spirit. It will have so many multi-dimensional expressions that it cannot be called simply an evangelism movement, a healing movement, a prayer movement, a unity movement or a prophetic movement. It will be all of those and more. Above all things, it will impart and renew deep affection-ate passion for Jesus by the Holy Spirit.

The Holy Spirit longs above all things to glorify Jesus in the human heart (Jn 16:14). He wants to impart deep holy affec-tions for Jesus in the bride of Christ. So for anyone to speak of this outpouring only in terms of a 'prophetic movement' is a much-too-limited concept. The increase of prophetic ministry in the local church involves more than verbal, inspirational prophecy. In my understanding, it includes angelic visitations, dreams, visions and signs and wonders in the sky, as well as an increase in prophetic revelation, even the kind given through the subtle impressions of the Holy Spirit.

My experience in the Cairo hotel room lasted only about thirty to sixty minutes, though it seemed longer. I'm sure many people from many places have had more powerful experiences. This experience took what I believed doctrinally about the ful-filment of the Joel 2/Acts 2 prophecy of a last-day outpouring of the Spirit and applied part of it to my life. I believe it related to this generation. This personal and contemporary application of a last-days dramatic worldwide visitation of God is without doubt based partially on my subjective experience. But more importantly it is rooted in my understanding of the Scriptures.

I left the room and walked around the streets of Cairo alone until about midnight, committing myself to the Lord and to whatever plans he had for me. The awe of God lingered in my soul for hours. I woke up the next day still feeling its impact.

The promise of Acts 2 and this experience impacted the way we started our new church plant in Kansas City. It is what initiated our commitment to intercession for a great coming visitation of God. The nurturing and administration of the prophetic ministry is a part of that and can only operate successfully in the context of building the local church. It is not an end in itself.

God's glory in the church

The supernatural events surrounding Paul Cain's birth, and his very unusual life and prophetic ministry at the age of thirty, I will discuss later. In the early 1950s, he was on television and radio, and had ministered in several meetings where 20–30,000 people attended. For his travels he purchased a tent which seated 12,000 people. But instead of releasing him to greater ministry, the Lord impressed upon him to withdraw from ministry for a season. That season turned into more than twenty-five years.

Paul struggled through those years wondering why God had set him aside in the prime of his life and, after such a supernatural beginning, seemed to have forgotten him. What encouraged and sustained Paul more than anything during those years was a recurring vision. Paul claims that it was like a cinema screen that opened in front of him, and that this vision happened many times.

I believe Paul Cain's recurring vision gives us insight into aspects of the great end-time revival that would be the complete worldwide fulfilment of the Joel 2/Acts 2 prophecy. In the vision Paul saw large stadia filled with people. He saw these overflowing stadia in cities all over the world. Great signs and wonders were taking place and countless multitudes were being saved as God's glory was being manifest in his church. In the last days, as in the first century, the increase of the prophetic ministry will not simply be a movement in itself. It is only one of the aspects of a greater and more far-reaching outpouring of the Holy Spirit on all flesh.

One of the unique things about the last great revival will be the signs and wonders displayed in nature, both on the earth and in the sky as described in Acts 2:19. I was awestruck by the personal visitation of God that I experienced in Cairo. I was surprised by the way God introduced me to the prophetic ministry. But the Lord was getting ready to overwhelm me completely by confirming prophetic words through the acts of God in nature.

3

Confirming Prophecies Through the Acts of God in Nature

The confirmation of prophetic words by the acts of God in nature is not a common topic in the church. But undoubtedly at the end of this age, signs in the heavens and the very forces of nature on earth will serve as a dramatic testimony both to the church and to unbelievers. In Kansas City, we have seen these kinds of things happen only a few times and know of a few other instances. It is, however, our suspicion that the church in other parts of the world might be experiencing more of this than the Western church. In the Western world, these kinds of events might receive much more publication and at the same time would be treated with more scepticism, as are all manifestations of the Holy Spirit.

When a balanced prophetic ministry flourishes, it is often followed by some form of signs and wonders. In his Pentecost sermon, Peter quoted the Joel 2 promise for a last-days revival. Of course, the last days began with the cross, the resurrection and the Day of Pentecost. The greatest fulfilment of these things will be in the final years of the last days, which are commonly referred to as the end times. That is, the few years just prior to the Second Coming of Jesus Christ. The first half of the passage speaks of the outpouring of the Spirit and the increase of prophetic revelation on the entire body of Christ.

> And it shall come to pass in the last days, says God,
> That I will pour out of My Spirit on all flesh;
> Your sons and your daughters shall prophesy;
> Your young men shall see visions,
> Your old men shall dream dreams.
> And on My menservants and on My maidservants
> I will pour out My Spirit in those days;
> And they shall prophesy (Acts 2:17–18).

The second half of the passage is dedicated to the great increase of the acts of God in nature.

> I will show wonders in heaven above
> And signs in the earth beneath:
> Blood and fire and vapour of smoke.
> The sun shall be turned into darkness,
> And the moon into blood,
> Before the coming of the great and awesome day of the Lord.
> And it shall come to pass
> That whoever calls on the name of the Lord
> Shall be saved (Acts 2:19–21).

There seems to be not only a connection but a divine order and sequence in the text: the outpouring of the Spirit, followed by the increase of prophetic dreams and visions, followed by the occurring of confirming signs in the sky and on earth. The fact, then, that we have witnessed a few of these kinds of supernatural confirmations in nature is related to experiencing the increase of prophetic ministry. We believe that what we have seen is only a small token of what will happen in even more dramatic ways in many churches throughout the nations. The last days will be accompanied by a multiplication of all four elements of the Joel 2 prophecy: (a) the outpouring of the Spirit, (b) prophetic dreams and visions, (c) signs and wonders on earth and in the heavens and (d) a whole-hearted turning to Jesus—first for salvation and then in 100% obedience and extravagant love for him. This whole-hearted calling on the name of the Lord is not only for unbelievers, but it includes the church growing in holy passion for Jesus.

First, this chapter is intended to encourage you about the future. In the end times, there will be awesome displays of prophetic visions and dreams with confirming signs and wonders in nature. These prophetic events will not simply take place within the confines of a few prophetic-type churches, but before the eyes of all mankind, believers and unbelievers alike.

As we have worked through the meaning of our own prophetic experiences, we understand that perhaps there are several reasons why the Lord gives confirmations of prophecies by supernatural acts of God in nature. People can really get carried away when things like this happen. We have painfully learned that the church needs to deal with such displays of power and revelation in a careful way. The body of Christ, in the process of nurturing and administrating this increasing prophetic ministry, will be faced more and more with prophecies that are confirmed by an act of God in nature. Consequently, a second aim of this chapter is to comment on what we have learned in the process.

The unexpected snowfall

A travelling prophetic minister had given a prophetic word to me in St Louis regarding the new church plant in South Kansas City before I moved there. In it, he warned of a false prophet who would be present in the early days of our new church. In March 1983, not long after our arrival in Kansas City, a strange-looking fellow introduced himself to me. I was at first sceptical about Bob Jones and thought that he was the false prophet I had been warned about. Ironically, on our first meeting, Bob Jones confirmed this prophecy by also warning me of a false prophet who would be in the midst of our new church plant. I wondered to myself, 'Can Bob Jones be a false prophet and then give a warning about a false prophet?' This thought was enough to keep me in turmoil for several days! I met up with the pastor of the church Bob had previously attended for several years. This pastor told me that Bob was a godly man and a proven prophet with much good fruit. He also told me that Bob had prophesied in the spring of 1982 that there would be a group of young people who were going to come to the south side of Kansas City by the spring of 1983, and that they would be used in intercession for revival. Therefore, the pastor blessed Bob's decision to join our new church of young people.

The first time I met Bob Jones was 7 March 1983. He walked into my office with a winter coat on. The reason this was strange was because the snow was long gone and the temperature was in the 70s in Kansas City on the day we met. During this first meeting, Bob prophesied that God was going to raise up a prophetic church in Kansas City and that he would be used in its foundation. He claimed that the Lord would confirm this prophecy with a sign in nature. He told me that on the first day of spring a sudden snow would come and at this time, he would sit around a table with the leaders of our new church, and we would accept him. I didn't take the prophecy seriously since I was sure Bob was the false prophet I had been warned about. I dismissed the matter, thinking that anyone who prophesied his own acceptance had to be a false prophet. But I still thought it was strange to see a man wearing a heavy winter coat during such warm weather.

Several weeks later, a friend named Art came to stay for the weekend. At the end of the Sunday morning service, I looked up and saw Bob Jones talking to Art. I fully expected Art to come over and inform me that I had a crazy man in the church. Instead, Art came back saying, 'Mike, this man seems like a prophet of God. He told me the secrets of my heart!'

Art had intended to fly back on Sunday after the church service, but his small private plane was grounded due to bad weather. At about 9.00pm that night, Art suddenly insisted on seeing Bob again. We all gathered at my house from 10.00pm until 3.00am. It was an incredible evening. I was overwhelmed at some of the things God revealed to Bob about private issues and personal prayers in my life. I suddenly blurted out, 'Bob, I'm thankful that Art insisted on our meeting tonight. I really believe that you are truly prophetic.' Bob smiled as he reminded me that he already knew we would accept him on the first day of spring, and that he had prophesied this the first day we met.

It was a true prophecy. The date was 21 March, the first day of spring. Art had been delayed by the sudden snow, we were all sitting around the table, and I had just accepted him with my own mouth. All of it happened just as Bob said the Lord told him it would.[1]

The unexpected snow on 21 March was predicted precisely by Bob to confirm the prophetic vision that God was raising up a prophetic church in Kansas City and that Bob Jones would be used in its foundation. The small but significant sign in the sky (heavens) was the prediction of a snow that would suddenly come exactly on 21 March, the first day of spring. This snow surprised Kansas City after several weeks of unseasonably warm weather.

---

[1] Marquis Shepherd, 'Gentlest of winters goes out with a blast of snow' (*Kansas City Times*, 21 March 1983).

The unexpected comet

A month had passed. I was a bit bewildered by the snow incident. We had continued to meet every night since November 1982, from 7.00–10.00pm, to pray for revival in Kansas City and across America. Then, on Wednesday evening, 13 April 1983, I had another very unusual experience with God. I heard the internal audible voice of God for the second time, saying something with unmistakable clarity. God told me to call the church to a solemn assembly of fasting and prayer for twenty-one days. The story of the angel Gabriel (Dan 9–10) coming to help against the demonic Prince of Persia was deeply impressed upon my mind. I also felt the Lord saying that people from all over the city would join with me in twenty-one days of prayer and fasting for revival in our nation.

I had some serious reservations about this. How was I, a new, young pastor in the area, going to call the city to prayer and fasting? Who would listen to me? The other pastors would think I was full of pride to presume such a thing! Diane wasn't very encouraging either. She was perplexed at the idea of announcing to a city that they would be invited to twenty-one days of prayer and fasting for revival. She reminded me that I had no credibility in the city. We had only lived in Kansas City for the past six months. Nevertheless, I was a little surprised at the resolve I felt in my own spirit. I was very new and perplexed at receiving these kinds of 'words from the Lord'. So the next morning, I decided to call Bob Jones (bear in mind that at this time I'd only believed he was the genuine thing for about one month).

On the telephone I said, 'Bob, I've received what I think is a word from the Lord, but it's pretty unusual. I guess I believe in prophets now, and I really need a prophet to confirm what I heard last night. Can you help?'

In his calm, drawling accent Bob replied, 'Yeah, I know all

about it. God has already told me what he told you last night.'

This seemed a little bizarre to me, but strange and unusual things were becoming more common. How could Bob Jones know what God had spoken to me? I had asked a couple of my friends to come along as witnesses, and drove to Bob's house. On the way, I explained to them that God had literally told me to call part of the church in Kansas City to twenty-one days of fasting and prayer. The passage I had received was Daniel 9, where Gabriel spoke to Daniel about the visitation of God. I arrived at Bob's house very anxious to see if he had really received the same message from God. If I ever needed a true prophetic word to confirm something, it was now.

I put Bob to the test. I asked him to tell me what God had revealed to me the night before. With a big smile on his face, he told me with great accuracy what God had spoken to me. My friends and I sat there in awe. Then he proceeded to explain several other things that God had showed him.

Bob said that he literally saw the angel Gabriel in a dream early that morning. He also prophesied that God had already given me Daniel 9, and that God was calling us to pray for a visitation from him for our city and our nation. In addition, in three weeks' time there would be an unpredicted comet that would confirm in the sky (heavens) that God was truly calling this solemn time of prayer and fasting, and that he was going to send revival to Kansas City and the entire nation just as he had told me.

We were astonished! I knew there was no way he could have known about the Daniel 9 scripture that I had received the night before. And the comet—that certainly would be beyond human ability. I thought, 'I wonder where this new prophetic journey is going to lead. I will just have to wait and see.'

Three weeks later, on 7 May 1983, the day our prayer and fasting began, the newspaper reported:

Scientists will have a rare chance next week to study a recently discovered comet that is coming within the 'extremely' close range of
3 million miles. . . Dr. Gerry Neugebauer, principal U.S. investi-
gator on the international Infrared Astronomical Satellite Project
(IRAS) said, '. . . It was sheer good luck we happened to be looking where the comet was passing.'[1]

So again, God gave a prophetic revelation that we were to pray
and fast for twenty-one days with the expectancy of revival in
God's timing, and then he sent a confirmation of the revelation
with a natural sign in the heavens—that is a comet was to come
across America on the day we were to begin the fast. That
comet was reported by the newspaper on the exact day the
prophecy had said—7 May 1983.

Signs in the earth beneath

Paul Cain, a man with a seasoned prophetic ministry, was to
have his first meeting with John Wimber, the leader of the
Association of Vineyard Churches, on 5 December 1988. He
went to John's home in Anaheim, California. A week or two
before Paul's pre-scheduled arrival, Dr Jack Deere, who was at
that time an associate pastor with John Wimber in Anaheim,
asked Paul if God would grant a prophetic sign to confirm his
message for John Wimber and the several hundred Vineyard
churches under John's leadership. Paul answered, 'The day I
arrive, there will be an earthquake in your area.' That, however,
is not an astounding prediction for southern California.

Jack asked, 'Will this be the big one we've all been hearing
about?'

'No,' Paul answered, 'but there will be a big earthquake else-
where in the world on the day after I leave.'

---

[1] 'Comet's path to give close view', *The Examiner*, Independence, MO,
7th May 1983.

The prophetic word Paul had received for John was Jeremiah 33:8 which says, 'I will cleanse them from all the sin they have committed against Me and will forgive all their sins of rebellion against Me.' Paul brought reassuring words to the Vineyard Church movement that God was still with them and that the word of the Lord was, 'Grace, grace, grace.'

At 3.38am on 3 December, the day Paul arrived, there was an earthquake in Pasadena, which is in the Anaheim area. Occasionally the Lord will use the timing (3.38am) of an event as an added emphasis to the prophetic message (Jer 33:8). I believe that this was more than a coincidence.

Paul left Anaheim on 7 December 1988. Another confirming sign from the Lord occurred the day *after* he left. There was a massive earthquake in Soviet Armenia on 8 December 1988, just as Paul had prophesied. There was no way that the fulfilment of such a sign in the earth could be brought to pass by human effort.[1]

John Wimber admits that previously he had always taken the possibility of prophecy seriously. Many of the major events in the development of the Association of Vineyard Churches were prophesied in advance. But Paul Cain represented a new dimension of the prophetic ministry that they had never encountered before. Concerning the effects that these earthquakes had on John, he writes, 'Paul Cain had my full attention!'

The Lord showed Paul that God would give mercy to the Vineyard as described in Jeremiah 33:8. God gives mercy and grace to enable us to begin walking on a more mature level of purity and holiness. The prophetic symbolism seemed clear. God was saying to the Vineyard churches through these events that he was going to shake the Anaheim Vineyard over the next

---

[1] 'Equipping the Saints', *Introducing Prophetic Ministry* (Fall 1989), pp. 4–5.

season by the prophetic ministry, just like the local earthquake that shook Pasadena. The prophetic shaking would not merely be local, but would eventually cause a shaking internationally. This was pictured by the internationally known earthquake in Soviet Armenia.

The mercy that Paul prophesied to the Vineyard in Jeremiah 33:8 was the prophetic vision that was confirmed by a sign in the earth. This sign in the earth (the earthquake) was symbolic of the shaking that the Vineyard would experience as God renewed his mercy to them during the season that followed.

Convincing power, irrefutable truth

Signs and wonders in nature are not to be taken lightly, because they are not given for trivial reasons. Don't expect God to show a sign in the heavens concerning which car you are supposed to buy. Fire fell from heaven and consumed Elijah's sacrifice, the Red Sea parted, and a star led the wise men to Bethlehem. These were not insignificant events in the progress of God's plan and purpose. The comet was *not* to verify something that related only to us. It was bigger than that. Our understanding is that it was to confirm to us God's purposes eventually to visit our nation with full-scale revival. We deeply appreciate the fact that God has used many different ministries over the years to prophesy and to intercede concerning the coming revival in America. No one group or denomination is more significant to God than the others. He does not move stars or part the seas to show off to curious enquirers. The magnitude of his manifest power is usually proportional to the significance of his purpose.

God's power displayed by signs and wonders in nature in the last days will be unprecedented because it will serve to confirm and signify one of the greatest events of all time—the last ingathering of souls and the Second Coming of Jesus Christ. The purpose of the outpouring of the Spirit, the increase of the prophetic ministry and, finally, the signs and wonders in nature, are all used by the Spirit to awaken the church to passionate Christianity and to bring people to salvation. The Joel 2 prophecy quoted by Peter in his first sermon makes this point with these words: 'And it shall come to pass that whoever calls on the name of the Lord shall be saved' (Acts 2:21). This applies both to believers calling with great passion on the name of Jesus, and unbelievers calling on his name for salvation.

All of this will be a great benefit to mature the church, as well as a dramatic display of power to touch the lost, for the last great harvesting of souls. It will be an extravagant outpouring of his mercy and power.

Convincing power and irrefutable truth marked the spread of the gospel in the first century. The presence and power of the Spirit provides undeniable evidence of the truth the apostles proclaimed. An important element of the gospel message in those days was that the apostles were eye-witnesses to the fact that Jesus was risen from the dead.

First-hand, eye-witness verification of this essential truth was of the highest importance in the initial preaching of the gospel. When the apostles assembled to choose a man to replace Judas, the stipulation was that he was with them from the beginning so he could 'become a witness with [them] of His resurrection' (Acts 1:22). One fundamental job of the twelve apostles was to provide eye-witness verification to all that Jesus said and did. Whenever the preaching of the gospel is recorded in Acts, you find words similar to this: and we are witnesses of these things. The gospel was proclaimed with convincing power and irrefutable truth.

The church's message in the end times will not only be that Christ is risen from the dead, but that his return is imminent. Throughout history there have been great revivals in which the power and presence of the Holy Spirit were so manifest that it seemed almost irresistible to some unbelievers. The ingathering of souls in the end times will be the greatest harvest of all time because the presence and power of the Holy Spirit will be accompanied with signs in the heavens and on the earth that will dramatically confirm the message of the gospel. This will be in a way that is similar to the apostles' eye-witness verification. Just as in the early days of the church, the gospel in the last days of the church will be preached with convincing power and irrefutable truth.

The Revelation of John is filled with passages that allude to the fact that in the last days, there will be signs in the heavens and on the earth given for the purpose of announcing the return of Christ and the ingathering of new souls for the great harvest. The events that occur when the Lamb opens the sixth seal are parallel to the signs and wonders prophesied in the Joel 2 prophecy (signs in the earth beneath, the darkened sun and the moon turned to blood):

> I looked when He opened the sixth seal, and behold, there was a great earthquake; and the sun became black as sackcloth of hair, and the moon became like blood. And the stars of heaven fell to the earth, as a fig tree drops its late figs when it is shaken by a mighty wind. Then the sky receded as a scroll when it is rolled up, and every mountain and island was moved out of its place (Rev 6:12–14).

In Revelation 11, John records seeing two witnesses and says of them:

> And I will give power to my two witnesses, and they will prophesy one thousand two hundred and sixty days, clothed in sackcloth. . . These have power to shut heaven, so that no rain falls in the days of their prophecy; and they have power over waters to turn them to blood, and to strike the earth with all plagues, as often as they desire (Rev 11:3, 6).

In Revelation 14 John sees one like the Son of Man with a sharp sickle in his hand. An angel came out of heaven and said to him with a loud voice: '"Thrust in Your sickle and reap, for the time has come for You to reap, for the harvest of the earth is ripe." So He who sat on the cloud thrust in His sickle on the earth, and the earth was reaped' (Rev 14:15–16).

It is difficult to know the exact interpretation of each of these passages, but it seems clear that the combination of signs in nature, the increase of prophetic ministry and the great ingathering of souls is spoken of not only by Peter in Acts 2, but in John's Revelation as well. In the Olivet Discourse (Mt 24) Jesus also uses the same language to describe the events immediately preceding his Second Coming.

> Immediately after the tribulation of those days the sun will be darkened, and the moon will not give its light; the stars will fall from heaven, and the powers of the heavens will be shaken. Then the sign of the Son of Man will appear in heaven, and then all the tribes of the earth will mourn, and they will see the Son of Man coming on the clouds of heaven with power and great glory (Mt 24:29–30).

As we approach the last days, there will be a great increase of the prophecies confirmed by the acts of God in nature. The greatest prophecy and the greatest sign that will ever be seen in the heavens is the last one, the actual appearing of Jesus Christ.

It shall not rain

On 28 May 1983, the last day of the twenty-one days of prayer and fasting, Bob Jones stood up in a group of about 500 people and gave a dramatic prophetic word. He said that there would be a drought over Kansas City for three months during that summer. The drought occurred from the end of June to the end of September that year. He went on to say that it would rain, however, precisely on 23 August. He said this was to be a prophetic sign to us that we should not be weary in waiting for the precise timing of the spiritual drought over the nation to end. Just as this natural drought over Kansas City would be divinely interrupted on a predetermined day, the spiritual drought would also be divinely interrupted precisely at the appointed time. Consequently, our fasting and prayer, along with the intercession of many others across the nation, was not in vain.

God wanted us to understand that there was a precise divine timing of the coming release of the Holy Spirit on the church in America and that this revival was strategically in his hands. In April of 1984, we received one of the clearest words that we ever received. God told us in essence that the spiritual drought in America would begin to end in the spring of 1994. He spoke audibly to two prophetic team members on the exact same morning. The message was clear: The wine of the Spirit would begin to be released in ten years. That would be in the spring of 1994. These things were all spoken publicly on several occasions to strengthen the intercessors throughout the mid-1980s.

Although prophesying that involves the withholding of rain is unusual, it is certainly not without biblical precedent. Elijah prophesied to King Ahab, 'As the Lord God of Israel lives, before whom I stand, there shall not be dew nor rain these years, except at my word' (1 Kings 17:1). Luke also records a similar event in the early church: 'And in these days prophets came from Jerusalem to Antioch. Then one of them, named Agabus, stood up and showed by the Spirit that there was going to be a great famine throughout all the world, which also happened in the days of Claudius Caesar' (Acts 11:27–28).

Apparently, prophetic ministers continued as a regular part of the leadership team in Antioch. Luke describes the young prophetic church in Antioch this way: 'Now in the church that was at Antioch there were certain prophets and teachers' (Acts 13:1).

Though the drought in Kansas City did not begin immediately (there was rain in the month of June), by the end of June the heavens closed. For the month of July and for the first three weeks of August there was almost no rain. By that time I had become an expert weather watcher, and I knew that on 23 August there was no prediction for rain. Much of the credibility of the prophetic ministry was on the line, as well as the fruitfulness of the twenty-one-day fast and the prophecy about the end of the spiritual drought for our nation. I doubt if anyone was as tense as I. Nevertheless, this thing wasn't my idea.

I called a friend in our church at noon. I said that it didn't look much like rain. He laughingly replied, 'You'd better hope it rains, or you'll have to leave town.' I couldn't see what was so funny.

Our church was scheduled to gather for a meeting on the evening of 23 August. Just before the church meeting began, there was a tremendous downpour of rain for almost an hour. Everyone was shouting and praising God. The drought immediately continued the next day and lasted another five weeks—three months in all as prophesied, with the exception of 23 August. It was the third driest summer on record for Kansas City in approximately 100 years.

While the unprecedented display of signs and wonders in the last days will be, in effect, the last and best invitation to the lost, the irrefutable confirmation of prophetic truth will also be a great source of encouragement to the church. It will enflame their fervency and passion for Jesus, strengthen their perseverance and enable them not to lose heart in the time of waiting or even suffering.

Because of this dramatic and unusual confirmation, we were greatly encouraged to continue to pray for the revival in Kansas City and in America, and not to grow weary as we are waiting for our prayers to be answered. The Lord also specifically spoke to our team about interceding for revival in the United

Kingdom and Germany and Israel. He spoke even more specifically about revival in London, Berlin and eventually in Jerusalem. The confirmation of the prophetic word by acts of God in nature has strengthened our faith to believe that just as the rain came precisely on the day predicted, the spiritual rain will come precisely at the divinely appointed time, even though we do not yet know when that will be.

Prophetic revelation and suffering

One principle to note is the connection between the abundance of revelation and a higher degree of suffering or testing. According to Paul, his thorn in the flesh was given to keep him from exalting himself in light of the abundance of revelation that he had received (2 Cor 12:7). The thorn was given *because* of revelation. On the other hand, it seems that God gives powerful revelation because of the testings that some are about to encounter. Paul received a prophetic vision instructing him to take his missionary efforts into Macedonia rather than Bithynia. That decision resulted in Paul and Silas being arrested, dragged before the magistrate, severely beaten with rods, thrown into the inner prison and secured in stocks. The clarity of their initial supernatural directions to go to Macedonia reassured them that God was still with them in the midst of their trial (Acts 16:6–24).

This revelation-before-tribulation principle is repeated many times in the Scriptures: the miracles of the Exodus before the wilderness testing, Joseph's dreams before being sold into slavery, David's supernatural military victories along with the prophet Samuel's words before the wilderness temptations and so on. Though the thorn can come because of revelation, so also revelation can come to prepare us for future testings. A powerful prophetic revelation with undeniable confirmations stabilises people in a time of severe testing.

In the end times, the awesome signs and wonders in the heavens will be much greater than these early experiences of the sudden snow, the comet, earthquake and rainstorm. How greatly will the saints who are awaiting the physical and visible return of Jesus Christ be encouraged by the undeniable confirmations of his coming!

Learning lessons the hard way

Our church unfortunately got somewhat out of balance on this. Many stood in amazement at these natural confirmations—the comet, the earthquake, the drought and so on. However, some people were unbalanced in that they idolised some of the prophetic ministers like Paul Cain and Bob Jones. Paul didn't ever live in Kansas City, but his reputation was bigger than life because of what happened when he regularly visited. The lack of balance in this area caused us to go through some painful but necessary correction. The Lord is jealous for his people and for their affections. He will not allow us to make weak and fallible leaders the source and focus of his work.

Some people may respond to this admission of our mistakes by saying, 'Ah ha! That's the reason we shouldn't get involved in the prophetic. It will only get us off balance and our eyes off Jesus.' I have had that argument with myself more than once and in doing so concluded several things.

First, I reminded God that involvement in prophetic ministry was never my idea. What happened to us was a divine ambush. We could only say, 'God, you got us into this!' It was an obvious sovereign orchestration of events.

We would have had to refuse the Lord to lead the church in such a way that nothing unusual, risky, prophetic or supernatural was ever welcomed or accepted. There would be less chance of people getting carried away, but the Lord would be grieved. I could have, perhaps, sought to minimise the ministry of the

Holy Spirit so that people wouldn't become too excited or emotional. However, a church that resists the prophetic dynamic can more easily fall into a spiritual rut. God ordained that the church needs the input of the prophetic to stay properly encouraged so as to minimise the unbelief and boredom that plagues so much of the church today.

Secondly, I am convinced that the outpouring of the Spirit, the prophetic ministry and the signs and wonders in nature are clearly a part of God's agenda for the end times. Whether we like it or not, what we have experienced is only a drop compared to the magnitude and the frequency of what is coming. This will become more obvious to the church as the Lord's return draws closer.

Thirdly, one of the most important reasons for embracing the prophetic is simply that the Scripture teaches us to: 'Pursue love, and desire spiritual gifts, but especially that you may prophesy' (1 Cor 14:1). 'Therefore, brethren, desire earnestly to prophesy . . .' (1 Cor 14:39) and, 'Do not despise prophecies' (2 Thess 5:20). It is easy to despise prophecies, and we are commanded by God not to allow such a mindset to dominate our church life.

Learning from mistakes

Because we believe that what we have experienced is only a small token of what the whole church will experience in abundance, it is worth sharing some of the insights we so awkwardly stumbled into. There are a few simple lessons we have learned about prophecies confirmed by signs and wonders of nature.

Number 1: Do not assume that such dramatic events mean that your church will be the centre of God's purpose and plan for your area. God is committed to using the whole church in unity in each area. Although we never bought into the idea that we were the only ones God would use, we definitely did fall into spiritual pride and became intoxicated by the 'heady wine' that this kind of revelatory experience can bring. That sounds simple, but throughout history people who have witnessed displays of God's power have concluded that their group was the central focus of God's plan for their generation. At Jesus' birth, the shepherds saw the angels sing in the sky and the Magi witnessed the moving star, but probably neither group was present to participate in the Day of Pentecost thirty-three years later.

These prophetic confirmations in nature were related to prophetic words concerning what God is going to do beyond the boundaries of Kansas City. We were allowed to witness the prophetic signs in order to strengthen and encourage our call to intercession for revival.

Number 2: Do not put undue emphasis on the prophetic vessels God uses. We gave too much attention to people like Paul Cain and Bob Jones. Some assumed that because they were so dramatically used they certainly must be right in everything they said and did. The Lord lovingly chastised us, because he is jealous for his Son to be the central focus. By the way, Paul and Bob are very different from one another and have rarely even spent time together. I have spent a lot of time with each of them, but they never connected relationally with each other in a significant way. Their personalities and ministry styles are quite different from each other. They relate to us differently and even believe differently on various subjects.

Number 3: On some occasions unusual revelation combined with extraordinary confirmation can be used to validate certain prophetic ministers. Such was the case with Bob Jones and the sudden snow in the spring of 1983. We feel that this was God's way of preparing us for some specific thing he wanted to speak to us about through Bob Jones. Even if this does happen, the church needs to proceed carefully. Confirmation of a man as a valid prophetic person is not a universal endorsement of all he says and does.

Occasionally, the Lord may give directions to a church that would be difficult to act on without a strong prophetic confirmation. One such event is recorded by Eusebius, the third-century church historian. According to Eusebius, the entire body of believers in the city of Jerusalem got up and left the city because of a prophetic revelation, and, consequently, their lives were spared: 'The whole body, however, of the church at Jerusalem, having been commanded by a divine revelation, given to men of approved piety there before the war, removed from the city, and dwelt at a certain town beyond the Jordan, called Pella.'[1] Immediately after their departure, Jerusalem was put under siege by Titus, the Roman general, and was destroyed in AD 70.

Surely God established the credibility of these prophetic messengers in the eyes of the church before the coming crisis. I don't know how he confirmed the prophetic message to leave Jerusalem quickly before Titus destroyed the city in AD 70, but I do know people aren't easily persuaded to leave their city and homes. So it must have been a strong enough confirmation to be believed.

I believe that there is a quality of prophetic ministry emerging in the body of Christ in our day that will achieve a similar kind of credibility in the eyes of both the church and, to a degree, even secular leaders and society. Many may scoff at this idea, but someday God may use prophetic ministry actually to save them from disaster!

The earthquake, the snowfall, the comet and the rainstorm were natural phenomena that we have interpreted as prophetic confirmations, because they were predicted to the precise day in

---

[1] *Eusebius' Ecclesiastical History* (Grand Rapids: Baker Book House, 1981), p. 86.

relation to a prophetic vision. Some think that these events happened coincidentally. The point of this chapter is not to provide lengthy data to prove the validity of these events in our experience. Rather, I want to highlight the fact that in the end times there will be undeniable prophetic signs in the heavens and on the earth, and that the magnitude and the frequency of these future events will far outweigh anything that has ever been seen before. I encourage you to think through what the Bible says about these prophetic signs in the last days. What exciting times lie ahead for the body of Christ!

4

False Equations About Spiritual Giftings

'It's too bad, Richard,' I replied. 'I'm sorry you feel that way, but it's true.'

My friend, Richard, is a dedicated and godly Nazarene pastor with an earned seminary degree. We are pretty much in agreement now, but at first he was absolutely shocked and offended at the idea.

Richard had an easy but inaccurate equation by which to judge spiritual gifts. He thought that a man with a history of accurate prophecies must be uniquely godly and biblically sound on most areas of doctrine. We disagreed. He had no experience with prophetic people, but had his theories clearly worked out. I had much experience with prophetic people and was receiving an ongoing education with regard to most of my old theories. Yes, prophetic people must be clear about major doctrines like the person and work of Christ and the place of the Scriptures. But on lesser points of doctrine, they might be very misinformed. One of the most surprising and enlightening things I share with conservative evangelical pastors is that there are people with valid gifts of the Spirit who are themselves still carnal. This challenges a commonly held idea that it is greater truth, wisdom and character that produce greatest power. Many think that it is only godly, mature people who are used by God in demonstrations of power, but there are many exceptions. What is often surprising to both charismatic and non-charismatic pastors is that people can express valid gifts of the Spirit yet have some pretty significant hang-ups and unresolved issues in their lives.

Many leaders have assumed that if there is a definite flaw in a person's doctrine, wisdom or character, then it is positive proof that the gifts and power in their ministries must not really be from God after all. Another false assumption is related to the way in which some look at Paul's first letter to the Corinthians. Since in that letter we find a lot of instruction about carnality, as well as the majority of Paul's instruction about spiritual gifts, they assume carnality must be the cause of the emphasis on spiritual gifts, or vice versa—spiritual gifts must have caused the carnality. There are a couple of things wrong with that conclusion.

First of all it is based on a faulty equation. Spiritual gifts are not always proved invalid by carnality. There is no suggestion in 1 Corinthians that the gifts being misused made them invalid. Notwithstanding the Corinthians' abuse of certain gifts, Paul adamantly continued to exhort them: 'Pursue love, and desire spiritual gifts, but especially that you may prophesy' (1 Cor 14:1).

Secondly, the suggestion has been made that since Corinth was the only church to which Paul wrote at length concerning spiritual gifts, they must not have been present in the other Pauline churches. The nature of the New Testament is such that you must be very careful how you mount an argument from silence, ie Pauline churches didn't know about spiritual gifts since Paul did not mention them in the letter he wrote to those churches. Most of us understand that Paul's letters were written to address matters at hand and were not constructed as a catechism. The thing I conclude from his silence about spiritual gifts in some of his other letters is that he obviously felt they were already in proper order concerning gifts. There was probably no need for additional instruction or correction on the subject of spiritual gifts in these other churches. Since Paul didn't mention the Lord's table in many of his letters, it might likewise be argued that none of the other Pauline churches knew about communion or practised it. First Corinthians is the only letter in which Paul mentions Holy Communion, yet it was undoubtedly practised regularly in all the churches, if not at most meetings. The abuses disqualified neither the practice of the Lord's table nor the practice of spiritual gifts. First Corinthians teaches us that valid gifts are not necessarily always a function of mature, wise and 100% doctrinally correct people.

Gifts of grace

The word used in the New Testament for spiritual gifts is *charisma* or literally 'gifts of grace'. In other words, they are given freely and are not earned. It was Simon the Sorcerer who misunderstood the gifts and power of the Holy Spirit, thinking they could be purchased (Acts 8:18–24). What a terrible thing, we think. No doubt Simon had a wrong equation, and Peter severely rebuked him because of the wickedness in his heart that would allow him even to consider buying the power of God. But there's not much difference between earning gifts and buying them. Money is only a function of effort and labour.

Contrary to some commonly held equations, the gifts and power of God are distributed at the will of the Holy Spirit (1 Cor 12:11). They are not given as a token or a badge of God's approval of the person's level of spirituality. Neither are they earned by our consecration. They are grace gifts. Paul wrote to the Galatians who had difficulties understanding grace and who kept putting law and works back into their equation:

'O foolish Galatians! Who has bewitched you. . .? This only I want to learn from you: Did you receive the Spirit by the works of the law, or by the hearing of faith? Are you so foolish? Having begun in the Spirit, are you now being made perfect by the flesh?' (Gal 3:1–3).

Apparently, the Galatians had experienced a filling of the Holy Spirit, and with it certain manifestations of spiritual gifts. Paul reminded them that just as being spiritually gifted is by grace, so justification is by grace. You can turn that idea around as well. Just as we are saved by grace, not by works of merit, we receive the gifts of the Spirit by grace, not works.

The lame man who begged for alms was commanded to walk in the name of Jesus by Peter and John. When Peter saw how amazed the people were over the healing, he said, 'Men of Israel, why do you marvel at this? Or why look so intently at us, as though by our own power or godliness we had made this man walk?' (Acts 3:12).

Peter wanted to make the point clearly and very quickly before there were any false assumptions. The manifestation of God's power was not a sign of his personal godliness. He went on to say: 'And on the basis of faith in His name, it is the name of Jesus which has strengthened this man whom you see and know; and the faith which comes through Him has given him this perfect health in the presence of you all' (Acts 2:16, NASB).

The healing was the result of God's purpose in his timing by means of faith in Jesus' name—a faith that comes through him. That passage contains many implications. But if it says anything, it is that the miracle was not about Peter or about promoting his spirituality. It had to do with God and his purposes.

Becoming the gift

Paul writes to the Ephesians: 'But to each one of us grace was given according to the measure of Christ's gift' (Eph 4:7).

What Paul says in the following verses makes it clear that the gift he is referring to is a *ministry gift*: 'And He Himself gave some to be apostles, some prophets, some evangelists, and some pastors and teachers' (Eph 4:11).

You can't help but notice the misconception about the anointed people referred to in this passage. We commonly assume that people are given the gift of being a prophet, pastor, evangelist or whatever. Paul saw it differently. 'He gave some *to be* apostles . . . prophets . . .' Clearly, the minister was a gift to the church. It was not an issue of the anointed gift being for the benefit of the minister. That really changes the way you might look at it. God's giftings are not about your promotion and esteem. God's gifts are distributed to people who become vessels and conduits of his mercy for the benefit of others.

The gifts of God in a person's life are not merit badges signifying the person's consecration, wisdom or 100% doctrinal truth. You might interpret the meaning of Ephesians 4:7 like this: Out of unmerited grace, each person is given gifts for the purpose of being used to bless others.

Gifts of the Holy Spirit, whether they are in the form of manifestations of power and revelation or in the form of people given as ministers, are for the purpose of blessing the church. Yet most of us can hardly avoid the temptation to see supernatural power-gifts working through an individual as a symbol of God's approval of that person's life, spiritual maturity and doctrine. The more significant the giftings and power, it would seem the more approval from God. If we understood that the manifestations of the Spirit are for the common good and not for the good of the individual whom God uses, we would be less likely to stumble over the idea that God uses imperfect, often immature people to bless the church.

By grace through faith alone

I am not suggesting an antinomian (lawless) approach to spiritual gifts any more than do those who preach salvation and justification by faith alone. I'm desirous to strengthen our conviction to examine all things carefully, even if they are from a famous prophetic vessel that is powerfully anointed. In his rebuke to the Galatians, Paul used the idea of receiving the gifts of the Spirit by faith and not works as analogous to receiving justification by faith and not works (Gal 3:5). In my mind there is a great difference between immature, unwise and even carnal servants on the one hand, and, on the other, those who are in deliberate rebellion and defiance against God. People in rebellion and defiance towards God should seriously be held in question if they claim to be used by the Holy Spirit in prophecy and healing.

This whole idea of grace is completely contrary to our natural way of thinking; that is, the gifts, even the gift of salvation, can be given on the basis of grace through faith alone and not with reference or regard to meritorious efforts. Outside Christianity, every other religion has at its core a prescription for some kind of salvation or union with God based on works. In this most commonly held false equation, man must earn his forgiveness, must strive diligently to bridge the separation between God and man. It is hard to understand it being any other way.

The point of this chapter is not justification, but giftings and manifestations of the Holy Spirit's power in the church. However, the same principle applies. There is no way anyone will understand justification by grace appropriated only through faith without looking at it from God's perspective. When you see the holiness of God on one hand, and the depth of mankind's sin on the other, a lot of things come into a new light that at first glance violates some of our formulas. Justification by faith alone makes sense only when you realise that there is no amount of human effort that could bridge the immeasurable gap. God's solution on the cross makes sense when you realise that the human effort equation is hopelessly flawed.

No amount of consecration or sanctification could earn the right to the gifts of the Spirit any more than indulgences could gain forgiveness, or Simon's money could purchase God's power. Gifts of the Spirit are given based on the grace of God, not on the maturity, wisdom and character of the vessel.

Consequently, we need to learn to recognise valid gifts of the Spirit in people's lives, even though they are a long way from being perfected. Careful nurturing and administrating of those gifts enables us to enjoy the benefit of the deposits God has made in the lives of immature believers. These deposits have been made for the purpose of blessing the church.

When compared to the purity and holiness of God, the differences between the best of us and the worst of us are not as great as some might like to imagine. The life and ministry of Jesus were, among other things, to show us what God is really like. Nevertheless, we still hold on particularly to misconceived ideas about God's ranking of sins. Throughout Bible times, God forgave and extended great mercy to people who, by our standards, did some pretty despicable things. Without diminishing the seriousness of some of the more serious sins on our list, Jesus showed everyone that God's opinion about things like pride, hypocrisy, treatment of the poor, unforgiveness and self-righteousness was more serious to him than we could have ever imagined. It violates some of our preconceived notions and the ranking of 'really bad sins'.

'Man looks at the outward appearance, but the Lord looks at the heart,' the Bible says (1 Sam 16:7). It seems he is rather patient and merciful with people who do bad things due to the fact that they are unwise, immature or just weak people. But to those who continue to disobey God deliberately, attempting to misuse God's grace and turn it into an excuse for sin, he often exercises his judgement to expose such deliberate rebellion.

The problem for us is that it is very hard to know what is really in someone's heart or how God perceives them. We need to be careful about judging spiritual gifts as invalid because of people's weaknesses and immaturity. God may be more concerned about what he has set out to accomplish in the life of the prophetic vessel than passing full judgement on that person.

False equation number one: Character equals anointing

Equations work backwards, even misconceived equations. Those who wrongly assume that spiritual giftings and anointings endorse character will also conclude that it is character that produces spiritual gifts. This encourages people in some circles to 'fake it' so as not to appear 'ungifted'. It also implies that the most spiritual, mature and righteous are those who have the most prolific gifts. If, as a church, you start down a road with this assumption, you are in for a bizarre ride.

This kind of thinking also sets people up for a great deal of condemnation, especially when everyone else seems to be prophesying, having prophetic dreams and seeing visions. I can say from experience that this can also put a lot of pressure on the people if they begin to feel they are less spiritual than those with greater gifts of power. I felt this way for a season and the result was that I abdicated my position of leadership to those with powerful prophetic gifts. The church was bruised and hurt by this decision that came out of my insecurity and false humility. Remember, most prophetic people don't have the gift of leadership which is essential for a church to be healthy, balanced and safe. A church led only by prophets is not a safe environment for God's people.

One of the most important things to do in a church that wants to nurture and administrate prophetic ministry is to actively discourage the mysticism and the carnal desire to look super-spiritual. We need to keep our eyes off people and remain focused on Jesus and his purpose for us. This is not a spiritual beauty contest, but it can turn into one very quickly if you see gifts as a merit badge rather than something to bless the church. It is not about the vessel. It's about loving the Lord and building up his church.

I do my best to make one point very clear to prophetic ministers associated with our church. The fact that power and revelation are flowing through them is not necessarily a sign that God is pleased with the other areas of their lives. Sometimes the prophetic gifts will continue to operate even when there is an inner crumbling taking place in their private lives. People with prominent spiritual giftings, as well as those with callings to leadership, must constantly guard against high-mindedness. High-mindedness is simply considering that you, your position or your purpose are so important that you are judged more leniently. High-minded people are those who consider that because they are doing such an important work for God, and because his power is manifest through them, they are not accountable for things like integrity, honesty and kindness—especially in the small and unseen matters of life. It is this temptation to self-deception that plagues many people in positions of power and influence. It is such a great deception because, in actuality, the opposite is true. To whom much is given, much will be required (see Lk 12:48).

Every person through whom spiritual gifts operate, as well as every person in a position of privilege or leadership, needs to be acutely aware that a day of reckoning is coming. Each of us will one day stand before God for a final evaluation of our lives and ministries (1 Cor 3:11–15). God has mercy on weak vessels and will manifest his gifts through them even when things are not totally right inside. But don't be deceived. This will not go on for ever. It's like a dog on a long leash. He can chase after a cat to a limit, but eventually and suddenly he'll come to the end of the leash.

Some of God's people have been displayed as examples of
God's patience with their sin and that his gifts are without
repentance. Others are examples of another fact that God eventually calls his servants to give account of their stewardship.
God's disciplines are manifest more openly to this group and it
causes us to fear God (1 Tim 5:20–24). Saul was a picture of
both ways that God chooses to deal with his servants. Saul
remained as king of Israel in his sin and rebellion, and was
patiently used by God to win great battles. God partially
blessed Israel under Saul, even with his sinful failing, but only
up to a point. Saul had lost the fear of the Lord and lost his
awareness that God was watching and weighing his actions.
Eventually he crossed the line with God. The message for
prophets, leaders and church people is this: God's gifts are
freely given as a sign of his mercy, not his approval. Don't disdain valid spiritual gifts manifested through spiritually immature people. But also, do not be fooled by God's grace and
patience with prophetic vessels who remain anointed for a season as they continue in their carnality. Eventually he will
undoubtedly call us all to account as stewards of the gifts he has
entrusted to us.

False equation number two: Anointing equals divine endorsement of ministry style

All the benefits that have come to our church as a result of the
prophetic ministry have naturally been accompanied by some
headaches. The greatest difficulties have had to do with ministry styles and methodologies. In a later chapter, I will talk
about some of the things that God does that seem strange and
unusual. He sometimes offends the mind to reveal the heart.
The point here, however, is the unorthodox style and methodology which prophetic people may adopt because of their own

weaknesses. I have had some long and painful discussions about this with some of the prophetic people in our church—from the most experienced to those just beginning to experience the prophetic gifts. In the most problematic cases, the people and even the particular prophetic word seemed to be anointed by the Holy Spirit, but their style of delivering it was really off. If you don't hold people to account, what begins as an unusual methodology can turn into exaggeration and manipulation. In several cases I have simply had to say, 'You must stop it.'

Prophetic people are often tempted to think that their particular method or style is essential to the anointing working through their lives. They will sometimes say, 'No, I have to do it this way or the anointing of God won't be manifest through me.'

Methodology or ministry style does not produce power or anointing. That's another false equation that some people fall prey to. Because you were standing in a certain place, doing a certain thing when God spoke or God moved or God healed, it doesn't mean the circumstances had anything to do with it. Nevertheless, people find themselves trying to recreate the setting so they can see God's power again.

The Lord often used Bob Jones by having him lay his hands on people's hands. He would sometimes put his fingers against their fingers and somewhere in the process, God would reveal specific things by the Holy Spirit that he wanted Bob to speak to that person. Bob Jones was consistently accurate in his prophetic ministry. Before long the finger-to-finger method became the way others sought Holy Spirit discernment for people. This is, of course, ridiculous. The discernment came from the Holy Spirit, not from the methodology. I've seen all kinds of people from all over the body of Christ imitating styles and methods because they begin to think that the method is the key. The person of the Holy Spirit is the key to operating in the power of God. We must constantly beware of thinking that if we get the early morning prayer meeting going just the way it was before, and the same worship leader back up there with those same anointed songs, then maybe God will do the comet-thing again. That's spiritual superstition.

Some prophetic ministers have these bizarre equations in their minds. The room has to be just such a way. The music has to be just right. There should be no crying babies who would cause the Holy Spirit to lift. It can get to be like a football player before a game, wearing the same socks or going through the same super-stitious routine. So what if the baby cries, or the room is not in the right configuration? What does that have to do with the per-sonality of the Holy Spirit and his anointing? The Holy Spirit is probably not as skittish and easily quenched by the lack of 'ambiance' within a particular setting as some people think he is.

What we call an anointed meeting often refers to creating and maintaining the right *mood* or *atmosphere*. Conservative Evangelicals can also do this. Some of them seek to know exactly which words and songs set the mood for the altar call. If the lights can be dimmed, that's even better. We all need to be careful to avoid thinking that methodology releases God's power or that the Spirit can't move without the right human methods. Music can be arranged in a way that is more enjoy-able and pleasant. It's OK to do that, but it is not necessarily the same as the blessing of the Holy Spirit or the presence of God. In some churches they turn up the amps and get the saxophone going, and, they will tell you, it is hot!

There is the natural tendency in some of us to try to systema-tise spontaneous experiences. Some think that if they discover the method-key, then they can control it. If you are successful in your ministry (or only appear to be), then you might begin to use the methods to manipulate people as well. I have had to warn some of our prophetic people to change their methods because they were basically manipulative and controlling, even though it was unintentional.

People who are perceived as anointed of God possess a

potential to use the power of suggestion. Here is an example of such suggestion and manipulation: 'Come up if you want to be touched by God. We are going to pray, and if you are really sensitive to the Spirit, you will fall under the power of God.'

Whether you are suggesting that people will fall down, get a prophetic word or speak in tongues, there can be a manipulative power of suggestion. I've seen a well-known minister rebuke people because they wouldn't fall down when he prayed for them. He said, 'Listen, just receive.' The lady replied, 'I am receiving.' But the minister said, 'Don't tell me you are receiving. You're just standing there resisting.' They got into an argument, right there on the spot. He really wanted her to fall down as a sign that God was touching her.

Ministers with power and prophetic giftings who are not in relationship with a balanced local church team often allow their method-as-power tendencies to dominate their ministry. It is simply much more difficult to get away with manipulation and pretence when you relate closely to a balanced team of people who live in the real world. Some people will push and lean until the person they are praying for goes down. To them it has become a personal vendetta because their public image is on the line. This is high-octane manipulation.

Miscalculations and false equations about methodology lead to hype and exaggeration. The methods become a false prop. The methods of ministry are operating in high gear, but in reality nothing holy and supernatural is actually taking place. The minister's credibility, however, is on the line, and he feels he has to produce. The sure proof of your formula or method is that it seems to work every time. If you've gone this far, you're already in the position where you feel pressured to say that God is working, even when he isn't. Whenever you move into that, you have crossed the line and made a critical mistake. You have started down a road of hype and institutionalised methodology. You are afraid to say that God is not moving in a particular ministry setting, because if you do, you feel like everything falls apart. There is too much vested interest in preserving the formula or the image. Some people build their organisations around the particular brand of methodology for which they have become famous. They take on staff, build organisations and have to keep the machine going. But one day everyone will finally realise and admit that the king has no clothes. Nothing is really happening. It has become a conspiracy of pretence.

The gifts and manifestations are given as the Holy Spirit desires. We can pray, dance and shout all night like the prophets of Baal, and if he doesn't want to move, he's not going to move. That is his business. God's surprise tests come sometimes by withholding his power in a key ministry time to see if you will humbly trust him instead of always appearing anointed. In his mercy, he gives us a spiritual quiz that reveals our motives, to help prepare us for the final exam on the last day.

We want to undermine the false equation which says that if you follow a formula, God will manifest his power every time. I believe that on certain occasions he strategically does not manifest his power, in order to win people's hearts away from the minister and his methods. Sometimes he will withdraw his Spirit in order to keep from perpetuating our confidence in methodology. Our desire is never to look weak, but Paul's testimony was that he delighted in weakness, that the true power of Christ might work through him (2 Cor 12:9–10).

There is a spiritual mystique that is intrinsically woven into prophetic ministry. After all, hearing directly from the living God about anything is rather an awesome thing. When open and hungry people are in the presence of a prophetically anointed person, they are both hopeful and fearful that this person will reveal secrets and divine perspectives to them. They often cling to every word such a person may utter. This dynamic makes both parties vulnerable to unique temptations.

However, I believe that it is a carnal thing to utilise any mystique that may surround the prophetic ministry in order to influence other people. Unfortunately, this happens all too often. Many prophetic people begin to take themselves too seriously, or they love the feeling of having such influence over others. They are tempted to make themselves look and sound more spiritual, holy and sensitive than they really are. I have observed and found that it is easier to get one's identity wrapped around the prophetic ministry more than any other role one may have in the body of Christ. Prophetic people often submit to others' expectations to be constantly hearing from God, whether God is saying anything to them or not!

I believe there is a sense in which we should make things a little harder on God when it comes to showing his power. I have pondered over Elijah pouring water on the sacrifices on Mount Carmel. He didn't put on lighter fluid and strike a match behind his back! He was confident that if the genuine fire of God fell, then it could consume even a wet sacrifice. I would challenge prophetic ministers to put some 'water on the sacrifices' they prepare and really trust God to prove his power without them feeling the pressure of trying to help God out so much. Then when his power is demonstrated, the people will not glorify the prophet of God, but the God of the prophet. I encourage them to throw a cloak over their prophetic mystique and deliberately refuse to utilise it to gain favour, praise, opportunities, sympathy, trust, affection or money. I appeal to them to stay impressed with God and his power without becoming impressed with themselves.

False equation number three: Anointing equals 100% doctrinal truth

Throughout church history there have been a lot of anointed people who came to hold strange doctrines. Their constituency bought into the false assumption that a person whom God uses in a genuine prophetic or healing ministry *must* be 100% doctrinally correct. The most notable example in recent history is William Branham.

Branham, a poor, uneducated Baptist, began his ministry in 1933. As a travelling evangelist his meetings were frequently attended by thousands, and sometimes over 20,000 people would attend. His ministry was characterised by an amazing manifestation of healing and the word of knowledge. Very often, when someone would approach him in a healing line, Branham would describe their disease, other unknown information about them and sometimes even call them by name. The gift, many people insisted, was 100% accurate. An interpreter for him in Switzerland and later an historian said, 'I am not aware of any case in which he was mistaken in the often detailed statements he made.'[1] The healings were also both numerous and astonishing.

Branham ended up in some doctrinal heresy, although never to the extent of denying Jesus Christ as Lord and Saviour or the authority of the Scriptures. This caused great confusion among his followers. They reasoned that if God could give him genuine prophetic information about people's lives, then why didn't God in the same way give him sound doctrine? The gift of prophecy doesn't in any way ensure that you will have the gift of teaching or vice versa.

The problem is that people with strong power and prophetic ministries often aren't satisfied. Being used by God in prophecy and healing miracles becomes almost mundane to them, and they often want to become teachers. They don't get a zing out of prophesying any more. One of the tough parts of prophetic ministry is that the essential ingredient in being effective is keeping your own opinions out of the way. On the other hand,

---

[1] David Edwin Harrell Jr, *All Things Are Possible* (Indiana University Press, 1975), p. 38.

the teacher has a platform on which he can regularly declare many of his thoughts. Prophetic people often chafe against this restraint on them that is not upon teachers. It is so important that prophetic ministers be a part of a local church team that includes gifted teachers. If they are not in a team, then they are in a place to be and do everything, and they often venture outside their calling. When prophetic people and evangelists become separate from the local church, they become tempted to establish doctrine as a gifted teacher does, especially if they have a large following. Some of the unbalanced doctrine so widespread in the body of Christ has come from such people who have a large following through television and radio. They teach multitudes who have been gathered by the supernatural gifts of the Spirit that operate through them. However, if they don't have a teaching gift that has been cultivated through proper training in the Scriptures, they are sure to teach unbalanced doctrine to their followers.

The most common example of this that I know of is the problem of 'gift projection'. Many anointed prophetic leaders have virtually conveyed this notion to their constituents: 'If you were really close to the Lord and sensitive to the Spirit like I am, you would be doing the things I am doing.' They have often failed to perceive the sophisticated and beautiful diversity of the body of Christ. In their attempt to encourage believers, they have unwittingly discouraged them.

There are a lot of pitfalls of which prophetic ministers need to be careful. In order to lend credibility to what they are teaching, there is the temptation to be unclear about authorisation. I've heard some people start out by declaring what the Holy Spirit has said to them, then immediately proceeding into their own ideas under the guise of prophesying. The problem comes when they fail to distinguish between a Holy Spirit inspired revelation and that which was their own teaching or opinion added to the revelation. Most of the congregation couldn't tell where one stopped and the other started. Pastors and teachers in the local church should watch that very carefully in the prophetically gifted ministers. Pastors need to be careful not to allow the presupposition that miraculous power and revelation validate the truth and accuracy in whatever else is said by the prophetic members of their team.

For the profit of all

False assumptions about spiritual gifts and what they signify will eventually cause you to throw out something good or accept something bad. Power gifts do not necessarily endorse character or methodology. Neither do the prophet's great miracles validate all his or her doctrine. The most important thing to remember is that 'the manifestation of the Spirit is given to each one for the profit of all' (1 Cor 12:7). Spiritual gifts are for the purpose of blessing the body, not to exalt the person through whom they come. An appropriate scripture for prophetic people to embrace and allow to govern their gifts is 1 Corinthians 14:12, 'Even so you, since you are zealous for spiritual gifts, let it be for the edification of the church.' God delights in using weak and imperfect vessels in order that he might receive the glory.

5

God Offends the Mind to Reveal the Heart

The introduction of prophetic ministry into our home church was difficult for me because I despised the weirdness of some of the people God used. I was also bothered by some of their bizarre methods, which were totally foreign to anything in my previous evangelical background and experience. It was not just the prophetic ministry that bothered me; other manifestations of the work of the Holy Spirit often seemed contrary to my sense of orderliness and respectability. Before I could move forward with what God was wanting to do with us, I had to deal with what caused me to be offended in my mind.

Some have created a lot of religious assumptions about how God deals with us. He is a gentleman, we say, who will never barge in, but politely stands at the door, quietly knocking and patiently waiting. The Holy Spirit is often thought of as being extremely shy or skittish. If we want the Holy Spirit to move, we stay very quiet and still. Some think that if a baby cries the Spirit might be quenched or perhaps scared off. This sounds ridiculous, but some Pentecostals and conservative Evangelicals alike operate under similar notions.

Paul's instructions to the Corinthians were that they should not forbid tongues or prophecy, but that they should 'let all things be done decently and in order' (1 Cor 14:40). Our leadership team has worked very hard at creating an atmosphere in which the free flow of spiritual gifts can take place 'decently and in order'. But Paul's instructions to bridle people who are operating in the flesh have been interpreted in such a way as to suggest that the Holy Spirit will only operate in ways that conform to our sense of order and respectability. That was not the case in the Old Testament, in the early church or in the history of revivals.

There are two facts that seem clear. First of all, *the Holy Spirit does not appear to be too concerned about our reputations*. The outpouring of the Spirit didn't do much for the respectability of those in the Upper Room. 'These men are not drunk as you suppose,' Peter had to explain in the aftermath of the Spirit's visitation at Pentecost.

Peter directed his first sermon not only to the out-of-town visitors who were in Jerusalem for the feast of Pentecost. Many of those were the people who were amazed and perplexed at hearing praises to God in their own language (Acts 2:12). Peter also preached to those who were the most religious of all, the Hebraic Pharisees of Judea, who being offended in their minds, mockingly said, 'They are full of new wine' (Acts 2:13). The disciples' behaviour might have seemed out of order to these religious leaders, but it was, nevertheless, the work of the Holy Spirit.

The second clear fact about God's dealing with us is that in contrast to the polite, shy, gentlemanly image we have of him, *God intentionally offends people*. It pleased God that the Gentiles were offended by the foolishness of the gospel message and that the Jews were tripped up by the stumbling-block of the cross (1 Cor 1:21–23). Paul warned the Galatians that if they were to require circumcision as demanded by the Jews, then 'the offense of the cross has ceased' (Gal 5:11). The implication is that the gospel is sometimes offensive by God's design.

The intentional offence

A good example of God intentionally offending people is in John 6. Jesus had fed 5,000 people with the multiplied fish and loaves. The expectation was that the Messiah would prove himself with some great sign. This 'sign' for which they looked was to be more than just physical healings, as phenomenal as that would be. They anticipated something comparable to the parting of the Red Sea, splitting the Mount of Olives or calling down fire from heaven. The people asked Jesus: 'What sign will You perform then, that we may see it and believe You? What work will You do? Our fathers ate the manna in the desert. . .' (Jn 6:30–31).

In other words, they were asking Jesus to do something like the manna-from-heaven miracle again. Jesus didn't give them their desired sign, but responded by saying:

> I am the living bread which came down from heaven . . . Most assuredly, I say to you, unless you eat the flesh of the Son of Man and drink His blood, you have no life in you. Whoever eats My flesh and drinks My blood has eternal life, and I will raise him up at the last day (Jn 6:51, 53–54).

Jesus offended them in their minds theologically by saying that he was the Bread that came down from heaven (Jn 6:33–35). He offended their expectations by refusing to give them the expected sign (Mt 12:39–40). He offended their sensibility and their dignity by suggesting that they eat his flesh and drink his blood.

The first response was that they 'complained about Him' (6:41). Then they 'quarrelled among themselves' (6:52). Even his disciples were baffled and said, 'This is a hard saying; who can understand it?' (6:60). Knowing their murmurings Jesus asked, 'Does this offend you?' (6:61). Because they were offended in their minds, even many of his disciples went back and walked away from the Son of God (6:66).

Throughout the Bible, God is revealed as One who offends and confounds those who think they have everything figured out; those who are bound by their traditions and expectations of how God operates. You might say they have 'hardening of the heart'. The words of Isaiah are quoted several times in the New Testament: '[He is] a stone of stumbling and a rock of offense' (Is 8:14). Jesus knew their hearts and that most of them loved their tradition more than God. He also knew that those who followed him in John 6 did so with mixed motives. He revealed their hearts by intentionally offending their minds.

By offending people with his methods, God often reveals the pride, self-sufficiency and feigned obedience that lie hidden in people's hearts. General Naaman, the commander of the Syrian army, was plagued with leprosy. He had come out of desperation to see the prophet of God in Israel. Israel was a military enemy of Syria. But Elisha only sent out a message to Naaman saying, 'Go and wash in the Jordan seven times, and your flesh shall be restored to you, and you shall be clean' (2 Kings 5:10). The prophet didn't even bother to come out of his house to see Naaman who had travelled so far. Needless to say, Naaman, a prominent military leader in Syria, was so offended by this that he said: '"Are not the Abanah and the Pharpar, the rivers of Damascus [Syria], better than all the waters of Israel? Could I not wash in them and be clean?" So he turned and went away in a rage' (1 Kings 5:12).

I know some obnoxious individuals who make it a practice to offend people. God's offence, on the contrary, is redemptive. He offends people's minds in order to reveal their hearts. The Bible teaches that God gives grace to the humble, but resists the proud (Prov 3:34; Jas 4:6; 1 Pet 5:5–6). Dealing with Naaman's stumbling-block of pride was the first essential step to his healing.

Offended at the people God uses

Paul wrote that God not only offends people by his message, but by his messengers as well:

> But God has chosen the foolish things of the world to put to shame the wise, and God has chosen the weak things of the world to put to shame the things which are mighty; and the base things of the world and the things which are despised God has chosen, and the things which are not, to bring to nothing the things that are, that no flesh should glory in His presence (1 Cor 1:27–29).

I understand that the context of this principle (God's intentional offence) relates to issues much broader than strange prophets and bizarre manifestations. But in these instances, the principle can be clearly applied. While I was still pastoring in St Louis, the idea that God offends the mind to reveal the heart became very real to me. I preached on it several times. I thought God was preparing us for an outpouring of the Spirit that might include some unusual things. I strongly believed in God's desire and power to heal the sick. I thought there might be some unusual healings. I had no experience with the prophetic ministry as I know it today. Actually, he was preparing me so that I would not stumble over the strangeness of the prophetic people I was about to meet in the months to come in Kansas City.

Compared to your average person working at the office, some prophetic people can seem pretty eccentric. It took me a while to get used to some of their idiosyncrasies, which greatly offended my mind at first. The truth is that some of their idiosyncrasies still irritate me, but I've learned to look past them for the sake of receiving God's blessing through them.

When I first met Bob Jones, I was completely convinced that he was not of God and I did not want to talk to him ever again. I had very little experience with prophetic people and no clear thought-out theology on the subject. Yet I had a firm conviction that he was surely a false prophet. I'm surprised at how authoritative I was about things of which I had no real understanding or experience. I think they call that pride.

Looking back I realise that one of the principal factors that influenced me was that Bob looked and acted so strangely. He spoke in parables constantly. I knew God spoke to us in parables too, but this was really strange stuff. Bob would tell me symbolic stories filled with word pictures for which I had no interpretation. Then he would claim that God had told him those parables. I didn't have any gridwork or paradigm in which God spoke in such abstract ways to people today.

Bob's ministry style was like nothing I had ever seen before. He would talk about feeling the wind of the Spirit, or how his hands would sometimes become hot during a ministry time. His language was that of an uneducated person. His appearance was such that no one could ever have accused him of vanity or of being too caught up in the fashions of the day. Occasionally his shirt and trousers were too short. Consequently, at those times, his stomach slightly showed when he stood, and when he sat, his trouser legs sometimes went three inches above his socks. He also had several innocent habits that I will not mention.

These things about Bob Jones somewhat offended me—his appearance, his language, his revelation and his ministry style. Initially, I could not imagine him being a genuine prophetic person and could not believe he was inspired by the God of the Bible. Only after I had seen the accuracy of Bob Jones' prophetic ministry over time did I finally begin to think this strange ministry style might be acceptable. His love for Jesus and the Scriptures also became apparent. Eventually, I found him endearing.

Offended at bizarre prophetic methods

Some people are different by their very personality and culture, but God has called them none the less. Bob Jones is a prime example. Others are led to do strange things by the prophetic call and ministry.

There is another prophetic person in our church who is pretty straight but, periodically, will do some fairly strange things. For example, once he grabbed someone by the shoulders and started interceding at the top of his lungs during a church worship service. Once he clapped his hands and fell down in front of a person. Most of these unusual actions represent some kind of prophetic symbolism. This kind of thing doesn't happen very often, but when it does, people in the congregation look at me to see what I am going to do. Once he fell on his face in the middle of worship and started weeping loudly. That seemed pretty bizarre to me. Afterwards I just told everyone, 'I have no idea what he was doing.' I later found out he was seeking to intercede for the church.

We all need to be a little more laid back and not so quick to pass judgement on things simply because they are unconventional or appear to be out of order (at least out of *our* order). At the same time we have to judge the fruit of this. There are several things to keep in mind:

Unbalanced people

Some unbalanced people are simply trying to be weird because of their misconceptions of prophetic ministry. They are excited about the idea of mystical prophets, and they intentionally act out of order. They suppose their strangeness will make them more anointed. I don't believe the idea that because someone is prophetic they should be strange or should be persecuted. People will try to get away with all kinds of things based on that idea, claiming that others can't understand them unless they are also prophetic. I don't believe that for a second. Some people enjoy Bob Jones' strange actions and try to imitate them because they think it's really spiritual, when in fact some of it is just his personality and upbringing. Sometimes the weird methods are just weird and it is not a case of God offending people's minds, but rather it is the prophetic person's offensive style and methods. Such things need to be gently corrected if these people want to function in public settings.

Remember that prophets are not always loners

The Bible speaks of 'schools' or 'companies' of prophets (1 Sam 10:10; 2 Kings 4:1; 5:22). This reminds us that there is a corporate dimension to developing prophetic gifting among believers. It is not necessary always to hear from God alone and then deliver his word in public. Other, maturer Christians can help those with less experience to sharpen their listening and discerning skills.

Unconventional ministry styles

Unconventional styles don't necessarily invalidate a prophet's message. Don't dismiss something simply because it is unconventional. There wasn't an Old Testament biblical precedent set for Paul to send out handkerchiefs to sick people (Acts 19:12), or for Jesus to put mud on a blind person's eyes. Jesus said we were to judge the fruit of a prophet, not his methodology, unless of course his methods violate a clear biblical text or principle (Mt 7:15–20).

If people have a track record for being accurate prophetically, you can take them more seriously when their methodology is a little unorthodox. Sometimes their 'methodology' is nothing less than following specific instructions from the Holy Spirit. It took some time for each member of our prophetic team to develop credibility with us. People without a genuine proven prophetic gifting do not seem to have as much latitude to do unconventional things.

Process of correction

As a pastor you have to be careful about correcting people too abruptly, especially in public meetings. We must deal with them in love first because they are important to God. If you don't correct them properly, the others will not feel the confidence to step out in faith to minister in the church. We go through a series of corrective steps. If someone prophesies something we discern to be fleshly, we will let it pass the first time, unless it is clearly unbiblical or destructive in nature. You need to give people room to make mistakes without fear of being too quickly corrected. If it happens again, then we will talk to them very gently and suggest they need to be a little more restrained. If they do it a third time, then we will tell them privately to stop it and warn them that we will publicly stop them the next time. If they do it again, we will confront the issue publicly.

We will then publicly explain the entire process we have gone through. This helps people to realise the correction was not an abrupt and harsh correction. We tell the rest of the congregation that this person was instructed and warned repeatedly. The others need to be absolutely assured that they will not be suddenly corrected publicly without prior warnings. Most of God's people really want to bless others in godly order. Communicating the whole process publicly keeps people from being afraid to step out in faith, and it also reinforces the fact that the church leadership will deal directly with these kinds of situations.

The 'now-ness' of the Spirit

Prophetic ministry cannot be an end in itself. Its purpose is always to strengthen and promote something greater and more valuable than itself. As I indicated previously, one significant impact of the prophetic ministry at Metro Vineyard in Kansas City was to strengthen our endurance and commitment to intercession for city-wide and national revival. People get off track when they allow themselves to become more focused on the unusual means of the message rather than God's purpose in that message. It is not so important whether the message comes from a five-star prophet with mountain-moving confirmations, or if it is something that simply seems good to everyone involved. The message is always more important than the method.

When I talk about nurturing and administrating the prophetic ministry in the local church, it is always in view of what God wants to accomplish through the prophetic, not just so we can promote prophetic vessels. In my experience, I have found that the very nature of the prophetic ministry is to alert the church to the 'now-ness' of the Holy Spirit. It awakens us to the will and purpose of God for us in the *present*—what he specifically wants to do in us and through us.

This aspect of now-ness is a complement to the other dimension of our faith and relationship to God which is for ever established, that is Jesus' work on the cross and the Scriptures. While prophetic people enlighten us to the 'now-word' (as some people call it), pastors and teachers should ground us in the word of God which is for ever settled in heaven.

I love both of these dimensions. I love doctrine and theology, especially theology about the loveliness and majesty of God's attributes. I also long for the manifest presence and purpose of God displayed in our midst by those more prophetically gifted. Who can be satisfied with static religion that works whether God is actively present or not? Genuine Christianity is both doctrinally sound and vibrantly experiential. The subjective side of our faith should always be scrutinised in the light of the objective side, but both are essential. God is always working to bring the word and the Spirit together. Someone has said, 'If we have the word without the Spirit, we dry up. If we have the Spirit without the word, we blow up. But if we have the word and the Spirit, we grow up.' Our desire is for *him*, not just knowledge about him. I am hungry for the fresh wind of God's Spirit moving on our hearts and in our midst.

So nurturing and administrating prophetic ministry in our midst is really only a secondary concern—a means to an end, you might say. What I am really concerned about is nurturing and administrating the free and fresh move of the Holy Spirit in the lives of all the people in our church. The problem is, as you are probably aware, you cannot predict, administrate or control the moving of the Holy Spirit. You cannot force your programmes, your preconceived expectations and your requirements upon the sovereignty of God that is manifest through the Holy Spirit.

Offended at the outpouring of the Holy Spirit

People are offended in several ways by the Lord. Some are offended by the message of the cross itself. Some are offended with the type of people God uses. Other people are offended by the way the Holy Spirit moves. I was not prepared for unusual manifestations of the Spirit, but I was even less prepared for the unusual people whom God joined to our team.

When the power of the Holy Spirit is poured out, it is sometimes in a way that is unexpected, and consequently it is ridiculed and rejected. In the first Great Awakening in America, as on the Day of Pentecost, a lot of strange things took place. In October 1741, the Revd Samuel Johnson, acting dean of Yale College, wrote an anxious letter to a friend in England. Johnson was suspicious of the revival then sweeping New England led by the itinerant preacher George Whitefield:

> But this new enthusiasm, in consequence of Whitefield's preaching through the country, has got great footing in the College [Yale] . . . Many scholars have been possessed of it, and two of this year's candidates were denied their degrees for their disorderly

and restless endeavors to propagate it. . . . We have now prevailing among us the most odd and unaccountable enthusiasm than perhaps obtained in any age or nation. For not only the minds of many people are at once struck with prodigious distresses upon their hearing the hideous outcries of our itinerant preachers, but even their bodies are frequently in a moment affected with the strangest convulsions and involuntary agitations and cramps, which also have sometimes happened to those who came as mere spectators.[1]

Jonathan Edwards' wife, Sarah, was also profoundly affected by the power and presence of the Holy Spirit. In her own words, she describes how for a period of time lasting more than seventeen days she would be so overcome with the presence of God, all her strength would leave her and she would collapse. Other times she could not restrain herself from leaping and shouting for joy.[2]

Jonathan Edwards was a defender of the move of the Spirit, but the extreme manner in which people were affected was too much for the conservative Christian leaders of New England. Their respectability was offended and they completely condemned the movement, primarily for the excessive enthusiasm and unconventional manifestations of the power of the Spirit.

Dr Sam Storms joined our staff in August 1993 as the President of Grace Training Center, our full-time Bible School in Kansas City. Dr Storms obtained a ThM degree from Dallas Theological Seminary and a PhD in Intellectual History from the University of Texas at Dallas. Sam was somewhat sceptical about these spontaneous outbursts by people who were supposedly influenced by the Holy Spirit. At the April 1994 Vineyard

---

[1] 'Samuel Johnson to George Berkeley, Oct. 3, 1741' in Stephen Nissenbaum (ed), *The Great Awakening at Yale College* (Belmont, California: Wadsworth Publishing Co, 1972), pp. 57–58.
[2] See *The Works of Jonathan Edwards* (Carlisle, PA: The Banner of Truth Trust, 1979), vol. I, pp. 1xil–1xx.

Conference in Dallas, his scepticism was removed. Sam was at the back of the room when the power of the Holy Spirit fell on him. He first began to pray and weep as the Lord was ministering to some deeper needs in his heart. Shortly after this he abruptly tumbled out of his chair laughing hysterically, although he was trying desperately to control himself. Long after the Vineyard Conference had ended, he was still incapacitated by the presence of God. Finally, it subsided and some of us helped Sam up and started for the car. But in the car park it happened to him again. Sam was repeatedly falling down and running the risk of ruining his yuppie clothes. Twenty minutes later we had got him into the car and to the restaurant, where it hit him again. We thought it was all over until we got to our hotel room and realised Sam was missing. He was stuck on the stairway, incapacitated by the power of the Holy Spirit.

The fruit of Sam's encounter with the Holy Spirit was renewed faith, greater reverence for the power of God, and what the Apostle Peter described as 'joy inexpressible and full of glory' (1 Pet 1:8).

A dignified Anglican bishop attended a meeting in Anaheim in 1984. I guess you would classify him as 'sceptical but open'. The Holy Spirit came on him that night in a powerful way. He was on the floor, crying and groaning and rolling. When he got up, his clothes were a mess, his eyes were red and swollen, but he felt himself filled with the joy and power of the Holy Spirit.

Blessed is he who is not offended

The Pharisees and the disciples both misunderstood Jesus and, consequently, they were both offended. We usually think of Pharisees as the really bad guys. Actually, they were the conservative intellectuals who were the defenders of the faith, who held to orthodoxy against the corrupting influence of Greek culture. But their stumbling-block was pride in the accuracy of their interpretation (tradition of the elders). They were content with their orthodoxy, but did not hunger for God himself.

The disciples were offended as well. Throughout the Synoptic Gospels (Matthew, Mark and Luke), we see an underlying theme of the disciples' profound inability to understand what was going on.

Those who were offended and who turned away from Jesus when he said, 'I am the living bread which came down from heaven' (Jn 6:51), were not Pharisees, but his disciples (followers other than the Twelve). Though he taught with great wisdom and did some mighty works in his home town, Matthew records that his friends 'were offended at Him' (Mt 13:57).

The most commonly used Greek word in the New Testament for 'offend' is also translated 'to stumble'. The Greek word is *skandalizo*, from which our English word 'scandal' is derived. God even scandalises his own people's minds. By offending people's minds, he reveals the things in their hearts that cause them to stumble. Jesus is revealed in the Bible as the Way, the Truth, the Bread of Life, the Door and so on. He is also 'a stone of stumbling and a rock of offense' (Is 8:14).

What is most revealed in the offended heart is the lack of hunger for God and the lack of humility. In God's eyes, these are two important characteristics of the heart.

Functioning in New Testament prophetic ministry and, even more broadly speaking, moving in the supernatural ministry of the Holy Spirit, is not an exact science. This challenges our improper control issues and our religious codes. It has been designed by God for this very purpose! True Christianity is a dynamic relationship with a living God and it cannot be reduced to formulas and dry orthodoxy. We are called to embrace the mystery of God and not to lust after neatly tying up every doctrinal or philosophical loose end that we encounter. Our hunger for a personal relationship with God himself should overpower this drive within us to comprehend perfectly every fact. Our humility before God should instruct us that we will never have all the answers, at least in this age. We're hard enough to live with as it is. As long as we're in this flesh, I don't think possessing omniscience would help us to be any easier to live with.

Self-satisfied religious pride

Jesus very directly addresses these root problems of self-satisfaction and religious pride:

> You search the Scriptures, for in them you think you have eternal life; and these are they which testify of Me. But you are not willing to come to Me that you may have life. I do not receive honor from men. But I know you, that you do not have the love of God in you . . .How can you believe, who receive honor from one another, and do not seek the honor that comes from the only God? (Jn 5:39–44).

These religious Jews were deceived by equating their knowledge of Scripture and their association with the religious community with the knowledge of God. Yet, truthfully, they were stubbornly refusing to enter into a personal relationship with God through his personal representative, Jesus. They boasted in their knowledge of Scripture while rejecting the Author of Scripture.

When the Lord was beginning to challenge Michael Sullivant to be willing to move down the pathway of his prophetic calling, he had a vivid spiritual dream that touched these issues in his heart. The Lord appeared to him, looked him in the eye and said, 'You have been waiting to obey me until you had comprehensive plans. I want you to obey me without comprehensive plans.' As Michael was kneeling before Jesus, a stack of transparencies came out of his belly and landed in his hands. He understood that these represented his own plans, which the

Lord could see right through. Michael felt chagrined and deeply sorrowful, bowed his head and began weeping and repenting. He was saying, 'Lord, I don't want to be disobedient to you.' After this, he looked up at the Lord through his tears and Jesus was smiling at him. To submit to this calling on his life, Michael has had to go through some rather stiff dealings with God regarding some intellectualism and self-reliance in his ministry and style of relating. This has included private corrections and even a degree of public humiliation to help him to humble himself before the Lord.

A few years ago, while functioning as a leading pastor at Metro Vineyard Fellowship, the Lord lifted the anointing for pastoral preaching and teaching off Michael for a while. This change was obvious to almost everyone in the church. This led to a shift in Michael's role, and he wasn't required to preach so often. A few days after this, Paul Cain, who knew nothing of this situation, publicly prophesied to Michael and his wife, Terri, that God's intention was to 'change his vocation' and lead them down a prophetic pathway. He assured them that the changes that had been occurring were not a demotion, but a plan designed to bring greater glory to God through their lives.

Any of us should welcome whatever it takes to enter into and enjoy a more intimate relationship with the Father, Son and Holy Spirit. The strategic stumbling-blocks that God puts before us in the gospel, and a walk in the Holy Spirit to test our hearts, can actually become the stepping stones that thrust us forward in his purposes for our lives, if we become hungry for God and humble in heart.

6

Embodying the Prophetic Message

Along with prophetic ministry comes the prophetic standard. The Lord wants his ministers to embody the message they preach, and will only 'wink' at their carnality for a time before disciplining them. We believe that the fierce controversy beginning in 1990 that surrounded Kansas City Fellowship (now called Metro Vineyard Fellowship of Kansas City) was authentic, divine discipline on our ministry and our prophetic team. Most of what was said by our accusers was inaccurate. They misrepresented our doctrines and practices, as well as using fabricated stories to validate their accusations. It was a terrible time of attack and turmoil for our church. That should not hide the fact, however, that God was disciplining us in several areas.

Embodying the message

God will often take his prophetic vessels and make their lives a prophetic illustration of the message they are called to proclaim. Ezekiel was instructed by the Lord to take a clay tablet, portray it as Jerusalem and lay siege against it as a sign to the house of Israel. He was to lie on his left side for 390 days according to the years of Israel's iniquity, then forty days on his right side for Judah's iniquity (Ezek 4:1–8). Sometimes God deals with his servants in a way that is hard for us to understand. That is one of the burdens of the prophetic calling.

By causing their lives to illustrate his point, the message-bearer embodies the message and also feels God's heart in the matter. The prophet Hosea is one of the best examples of this. God instructed him to embrace and marry a harlot. In doing so, Hosea demonstrated God's love and forbearance towards the harlot nation of Israel. This was undoubtedly a painful thing for Hosea, but it enabled him to feel the heart of God (Hos 3).

God wants his servants not only to *say* what he is like, but to *be* like him; not only to *say* what he wants, but to *do* and *demonstrate* his will; not only to *declare* his heart, but to *feel* his heart.

The true nature of prophetic ministry, in my way of thinking, is passion for the heart of God. The Apostle John records the angel saying to him, 'Worship God! For the testimony of Jesus is the spirit of prophecy' (Rev 19:10). Bringing the fresh revelation of the heart of Jesus (the testimony of Jesus) to us is the focus and motivation of the prophetic ministry. It involves more than simply communicating his ideas. It is feeling and revealing his heart.

The Lord spoke audibly to two members of our prophetic team on the same morning in April 1984. In essence, he said that he had placed an emphasis and requirement of humility upon the leadership of the church. Most of us at Metro Vineyard, of course, thought of it in terms of emphasising the *doctrine of humility* without really considering the implementing of it in our everyday lifestyle. For God to speak audibly to two people at the same time, you would think we'd have taken the message to heart in the fullest way possible. But God was also referring to the fact that he would dramatically confront our pride and selfish ambition. One way in which the Lord did this was by allowing us to be severely mistreated and then requiring us to bless our enemies. In this, we saw degrees of pride and selfish ambition in our hearts that we never imagined possible. The reason for that, as I see it now, is that he wants us not only to preach the doctrine of humility that resists selfish ambition, but to be living demonstrations of the message. If you're going to preach it, you have to live it. We haven't done a very good job at demonstrating humility, but it is something God will continue to deal with in us throughout the coming years.

Thorns in the flesh

When God communicates a purpose and message to you with dramatic supernatural manifestations (angelic visitations, audible voices and signs in the heavens), then know the Lord is urgent about making it apply to your life, and if necessary he will deal severely with you on those issues. God will challenge the areas in our lives that are inconsistent with the message he has given us to proclaim. Also, as we have seen, God sends a thorn in the flesh to those whom he gives abundant revelation so as to protect their hearts from destructive pride. The Apostle Paul said that he had been given a 'thorn in the flesh' in order that he would not exalt himself. This was due to the fact that his ministry was surrounded by an 'abundance of the revelations' (2 Cor 12:7).

God has purposed to work through each of us a life message. Sometimes the inner working of the Holy Spirit is carried out for almost a lifetime before that person is ever given the full platform to release the message. With others, the beauty of God's work in them is never put on a public stage and is perhaps seldom noticed, except by a few. In such a case, it is, nevertheless, perfected in a person's life for God's pleasure and the impact of individuals around them. Still there are others who are called to be proclaimers of the message. Some have been given an early platform and are allowed to preach beyond the maturing work of the Holy Spirit in their lives. I came to discover that, to one degree or another, that has been our situation. We were called to proclaim a message of humility that we ourselves did not yet possess. The discipline of the Lord was then released to equip our hearts in purity and humility.

God's desire for all of us is that we would examine ourselves carefully in the light of his word and be sensitive to the Holy Spirit's conviction in areas that need to change. But, eventually, if we don't recognise the problems and deal with them, there are all kinds of external circumstances that can be used to bring to light the unresolved or carnal issues in our lives. The thorn in the flesh produces humility over time in the lives of sincere yet immature followers of Christ Jesus. The Scriptures suggest in several places that God extends his grace to people and patiently waits for them to change. Here are a few examples:

> Truly, these times of ignorance God overlooked, but now commands all men everywhere to repent, because He has appointed a day on which He will judge the world. . . (Acts 17:30–31).

> Do you despise the riches of His goodness, forbearance, and long-suffering, not knowing that the goodness of God leads you to repentance? (Rom 2:4).

> The Lord is not slack concerning His promise, as some count slackness, but is longsuffering toward us, not willing that any should perish but that all should come to repentance (2 Pet 3:9).

If we really love God, he gives us the chance to voluntarily respond to the Spirit, but if we don't respond, he will most often extract submission from us. The prophetic controversy we were about to find ourselves in the middle of was (in retrospect) God's way of extracting that kind of compliance. God was forcing an issue with us—that we would embody the message we were called to proclaim.

Watching the wrong gauges

In 1989, we seemed to be eating with a golden spoon. I was travelling with John Wimber and speaking regularly to crowds of thousands of people at international conferences. After a while I grew tired of it physically and emotionally. However, I enjoyed the attention and honour more than I knew. People loved the messages and queued up to buy our tapes. I was meeting prominent Christian leaders from different nations. One of them said that what was happening in Kansas City was the freshest thing in a decade. My pride was being stroked and strengthened. I was overwhelmed with the invitations to preach and requests for interviews. A dozen publishers wanted me to write books for them. Several companies sent proposals to distribute our tapes in their nation. It was physically impossible to answer the multitudes of letters and phone calls that came monthly. We were completely overwhelmed and in over our heads. We complained about the pressures, but actually our team enjoyed the attention more than we cared to admit. We were out of touch with our pride, our limitations and exactly what it was that God wanted to do in us.

For a short while, whatever we touched seemed to prosper, so we figured God was excited about everything just as it was. There were, however, some warning signals, but we were moving too fast to recognise them. One problem was that in our early stages of growth we didn't have enough spiritual maturity to discern some basic warnings about our pride. If someone had said, 'You have pride,' we would have gone overboard 'repenting' of pride. But I don't believe we would actually have seen our pride from God's perspective, or even from the perspective of other people.

One of the warning signs we missed was that we were 'partying alone'. We were so happy about the seemingly great things that were beginning to happen in the midst of our ministry that we didn't even notice that some other ministries were not having such a great time. We were rejoicing in our increase, but we ignored the fact that other ministries were having a difficult time. Meanwhile, we partied on. We didn't see or feel their pain. We only saw our increase. If another church struggled or even disbanded, it was no concern to us, as long as we continued to grow and increase. We now lament over our having been so self-absorbed. Currently, we are more aware of these sinful tendencies in our hearts than we were in our early days.

We now have more of a burden for other congregations in our city. We don't want to celebrate alone. When the Lord says that he is going to visit us, we ask, 'But what about the other churches in the city? Are you going to visit them too?' We need to have Moses' point of view. God told Moses that he would make from Moses' descendants a great nation after he first destroyed the nation of Israel. Perhaps that was a test for Moses. Whatever the case, Moses pleaded with the Lord to forgive the sins of the Children of Israel (Ex 32). Moses had no desire to see Israel destroyed and himself made the head of a new nation. A Moses-type leader would intercede until God included more of his people in the blessing. On the other hand, Elijah didn't ask God to extend mercy to others, but declared that he was the only faithful servant left and wondered why God did not treat him better (1 Kings 19). The same is true for Jonah, who was bitter at God for extending his mercy to the Ninevites (Jon 4). A major warning sign we missed was that we felt no desire to include others because we were completely satisfied as long as our ministry was being blessed. That revealed a deeply ingrained pride and self-centredness.

The second warning sign was related to our lack of perception that we needed other ministries. There were a lot of people around the body of Christ who had much to contribute to what we were doing, but we didn't realise our need of their insight and input. They could have showed us how to do a lot of things better, but we were too busy and too caught up in the euphoria of our seemingly early success.

There were other warning signs that we missed back then and no doubt some that we still haven't discerned.

The temptations of opposition

Things seemed to be going so well through 1989, but in January 1990, it suddenly changed. It was as if we tripped a bomb wire when we stepped into the 1990s, for we were soon being aggressively attacked by ten to twelve different ministries. To our knowledge, none of these ministries were connected and, for the most part, they didn't even know each other. Most of them were passing along lies about our doctrines and practices and presenting us as an extreme cult group that was deceived by demons. It was terribly humiliating.

In the midst of this painful situation, there were two main issues; two temptations we had to face regarding how we would respond to these people.

At first there was the *temptation to retaliate*. We had people from several places encouraging us to stand up and set the record straight. This would involve revealing certain negative things about these groups. We were not comfortable spending our time and resources on attacking other Christians. Many people felt it was our responsibility to 'defend the purpose of God'. Deciding what to do was a difficult struggle among our staff, but there were several factors that helped us decide to remain silent.

Years before, the Lord had told several prophetic people through dreams and visions that we would face this controversy. In September 1984, the Lord plainly revealed to us who one of the principal accusers would be. The Lord added that we were not to strike back. At that same time, the Lord even told us when the attack would take place. Five years later, in December 1989, some of our staff pastors discussed the fact that an attack would probably soon follow since the time God had spoken about had now arrived. The attacks started immediately in January 1990. The fact that we had this information on the back burner for just over five years helped us to know that God was in control.

We also had some good advice. Early on the prophetic people had spoken very clearly about how this would happen and what our response should be. But it was John Wimber whose advice impacted our decision in the very hour it happened. John used the illustration of Solomon and the two women claiming to be the mother of the same child. When Solomon pretended he was about to divide the child with a sword, the true mother gave up her rights to the baby and allowed the lying woman to have the child. In this the true mother was revealed (1 Kings 3:16–28). John said that if we really cared about the bigger purpose of God, we would not retaliate. It would only create a destructive fury, and the purpose of God (the child) would be divided.

It was in our anger and desire for revenge that we discovered our selfish ambition. The things that were being said were significantly false, and I was growing increasingly angry. About that same time I received a clear communication from the Lord. He said, 'The measure of your anger towards these men is the measure of your unperceived ambition.' I reacted and said out loud, 'No! It's not my unperceived ambition. Lord, I care about your kingdom and your name being defamed.' Then the Lord asked me a question: 'Why then aren't you this angry when my name gets defamed when other ministries are maliciously attacked?' I had to be honest and admit that I was not mad when other Christian leaders were being criticised. It was the blow to my reputation that really bothered me. I saw with greater clarity that I had a selfish agenda that I was afraid might be hindered if the attacks persisted.

After struggling with it for a while, I realised that what the Lord had said was very true: *The measure of my anger towards these men was the measure of my unperceived ambition.* We were inaccurately monitoring our ministry by the gauge of numerical and financial success. But now I realised that there was an important indicator to which we had paid little attention. There was a fault line of selfish ambition hiding beneath our surface. Just as earthquakes expose the fault lines that lie deep below the surface, so also the current pressures on us were exposing our hidden fault lines of ambition and anger. We only had to be honest enough to admit it.

The true gauges of successful ministry are those issues that pertain to our becoming Christlike. Was our heart growing in tender affection for Jesus? Were we growing in our ability to endure hardship out of love? Could we bless our enemies with joy? These are the issues that God wants the prophetic ministry to successfully impart. We discovered that we were not very successful by God's gauges.

Secondly, there was the *temptation to say that the attacks were all of the devil.* In retrospect, we see that God's hand was in all of this—even using the things that came from Satan's hand as well. Most of the accusations were drawn from inaccurate information. The methods used by our accusers were often unrighteous. There was tension in our church body as we tried to decide whether the critics were totally misguided or partially right. Our present conclusion is that it was some of both. The lack of wisdom and humility in us provoked certain things in them. In addition to that, some of the things they were pointing out were true—especially regarding our pride. In any case, the uproar that ensued stopped us in our tracks and forced us to confront some of our problems. In that sense, we have come to see the redemptive hand of God in the whole mess.

There is a great danger in blaming everything on the devil. Some immature prophetic people tend to have a persecution complex. They feel the very nature of their calling means they are going to be persecuted. Consequently, whenever a genuine word of correction comes, some may bristle and think to themselves, 'Yes, we expected this because true prophets are always persecuted.'

I know of a large Christian group that was being harshly criticised by what some call 'cult watchers' and 'heresy hunters'. It seems the methods and most of the data used against them were in fact questionable. The Christian ministry concerned determined that the critics were from the devil and were simply persecuting the move of God. But because of this initial perception that the critics were solely the devil's instruments of persecution, the group didn't receive the divine correction. It has since disbanded over the very issues that were being pointed out to it by the cult watchers. Though they still see the methods used against them as inappropriate, many of the leaders of that organisation now admit that some of the things they were accused of were accurate and, perhaps, were God's way of bringing correction.

Six lessons learned the hard way

God used this painful series of events to bring correction to us in several ways. It didn't do a whole lot for our reputation, but I've learned that God is more concerned that we embody the message than he is about preserving our reputation.

The first area of correction was definitely pride. We were caught up in the early increase and popularity of our ministry. God can change that pretty quickly. Some of the things we said came out sounding as if we were the spiritually élite. John Wimber confronted our 'know it all' attitude, and we eventually agreed with our critics that we wrongly desired to be the centre of some of the revival we prophesied about.

The second area of correction was that we should recognise

our desperate need for other ministries in the body of Christ who were very different from us. If I ever doubted there were spiritual fathers in America, I found them through this. A number of older mature men of God spoke into our situation. We grew to appreciate deeply parts of the body of Christ that we had no real honour for in our earlier days, receiving edifying input from Anglicans, Presbyterians, Baptists and non-denominational streams. For years John Wimber has taught the Vineyard pastors to 'love the whole church', not just those who look and act like us.

A third correction was that we must have greater wisdom and understanding of the prophetic process. We had an immature and naïve view of the prophetic ministry. We underestimated the fact that it can have negative as well as positive effects. We also found some elements of manipulation and control in some of our team. Some of us were brokering revelational knowledge with an attitude of spiritual pride, for which we are now regretful. This can be very painful and even destructive to people's faith. Inappropriate expectations were, in some instances, sown into people through inaccurate interpretation and the resulting application of prophetic revelations. It revealed a lack of wisdom and a great need for a more mature administration of the prophetic ministry in our midst.

Fourthly, we had to change our concept of the city-wide church. We had taught that the entire city would come under one governing eldership. We put too much emphasis on structure as the basis of future unity. We now focus on city-wide unity through relationship instead of through structure.

The fifth correction had to do with accountability. We saw our need for input from people who had authority to correct us. As a result, we at Kansas City Fellowship submitted ourselves to John Wimber's oversight and became a part of the Association of Vineyard Churches. A couple of the prophetic ministers moved to the leading church in Anaheim for more theological training and oversight. I strongly believe in the need for all churches and travelling ministries to be accountable to people both inside and outside of their immediate local setting.

Under John's direction, we put some restraints on Bob Jones. The purpose was to set some safe boundaries with regard to things he would say publicly. Bob didn't agree and, consequently, was less than diligent in staying within those restraints. There were some other problems that followed in Bob's life which caused John Wimber to place Bob under a season of discipline. Bob moved from Kansas City to fulfil that season, and I understand he is doing much better. He is ministering again, but is no longer under the covering of our church here or the Vineyard movement.

The sixth correction was that we needed to have a balanced team. In every church there needs to be balanced input to maintain the stability as well as zeal and motivation within the church. We all need the high-octane prophetic people with more unusual supernatural manifestations, but we also need the dedicated theologians and the compassionate pastors as well as all the other ministries. You don't need to have a full-time prophetic minister on your staff to have the benefit of the prophetic ministry. We can often help local churches locate a proven prophetic team to visit them. Some ministries provide stability to a church and others, like the prophetic ministries, add zeal and motivation. Some contribute by inspiring people to greater devotion to the Lord.

My ministry is certainly not characterised by any unusual power or prophetic giftings, nor am I a theologian. My focus is inspirational in nature. I specifically seek to stir up renewed love for Jesus in the churches I visit. Locally, we have several theologians on our staff who relate with our prophetic ministers. Currently, we have four people with earned doctorates and eight with master's degrees from various conservative evangelical seminaries. We must diligently seek to integrate these trained teachers with prophetic ministers. I feel very strongly about this. It is not easy, but it is vital to see this diversity in the churches. Alongside these seminary-trained pastors and teachers, we have a fluctuating number of prophetic people and gifted musicians. This combination is very necessary, but at times very turbulent. I mention the musicians because they are absolutely vital to cultivating a prophetic church and can sometimes be as great a challenge to pastor as the prophetic people. (We shall look at music in more detail later.) The continual challenges of integrating such diverse people are well worth the tremendous benefit they bring to the church community. Remember, the whole team doesn't need to live in one city. You can cultivate this diversity by having travelling ministries come to your church on a somewhat regular basis.

The discipline of the Lord

Hebrews 12:3–15 is a very important passage in the New Testament.

> For consider Him who endured such hostility from sinners against Himself, lest you become weary and discouraged in your souls. You have not yet resisted to bloodshed, striving against sin. . .My son, do not despise the chastening of the Lord, nor be discouraged when you are rebuked by Him; for whom the Lord loves He chastens, and scourges every son whom He receives . . . lest any root of bitterness springing up cause trouble, and by this many become defiled.

This scripture points out the two obvious carnal reactions and then another more subtle reaction to the redemptive disciplines of God in our lives. The first wrong response is to despise his correction by embracing some form of denial concerning our need for adjustment. We despise God's discipline when we think of all of our problems as only being the attack of Satan without any regard for God's redemptive discipline. Thus, we regard his discipline too lightly. The second carnal reaction is to be discouraged under his loving reproof and fall into paralysing self-condemnation and hopelessness. Those who become discouraged by God's redemptive disciplines decide to cease following hard after God. It is too painful and the cost is too great. They decide that it is no longer worth it. Both of these extremes speak of a spiritual immaturity which we desperately need to outgrow. The third is to become embittered at God for his dealings in our lives. This is probably the most dangerous reaction of all, for bitterness is a deadly spiritual poison that also deeply affects all our relationships.

I don't think contemporary Western Christians typically relate in a healthy way to the discipline of the Lord. Very few people I know have had positive disciplinary experiences with the primary earthly authority figures in their personal histories. It is natural to transfer our experiences with such people to the Lord and thereby get a warped image of who he is and what he is really like. It is challenging for some to believe not only that God loves us, but that he also likes us and enjoys us, even in our immaturity. Many people actually give up on their walk with the Lord because of their misconceptions regarding his nature. This is why it is crucial to meditate on what the Scripture teaches about the personality of God.

We must seek the higher ground of responding properly to the dealings of God in our lives. We need to learn to take our medicine humbly in the proper ways at the proper times without becoming bitter and angry at God. We mustn't be either insensitive or hyper-sensitive when our loving heavenly Father points out our faults and errors. By the way, according to this passage, one of the primary ways in which God disciplines us is by allowing us to experience injustices at the hands of others. He allows us to be tested and is watching for a response of trust in him and forgiveness towards our offenders. The Proverbs state that 'the ways of reproof are the ways of life'. May God help us to learn how to honour him when we go through our necessary times of discipline.

Remember that the purpose of God's discipline is to equip our hearts in Christlikeness. Hebrews 12:10 says it clearly: 'God disciplines us for our good, that we may share in his holiness' (NIV). The prophetic message that he gives us is in essence to embrace the various dimensions of Christlikeness. His overall prophetic goal for all Christians is 'to be conformed to the image of His Son' (Rom 8:29). God wants us to embody the prophetic message that he entrusts to us. It is never enough to proclaim a message. We must seek to live the message we proclaim before we can genuinely claim to have a prophetic message and a prophetic ministry. In one sense, God wants his word to become flesh in our lives. Therefore, he sends various forms of redemptive discipline to help us see the unperceived weaknesses in our lives, those hidden fault lines beneath the surface. We can despise those disciplines and decide to stop pursuing the Lord as fervently as we once did. We can be bitter at God for allowing discipline. Or we can respond in the only right way, which is to endure his redemptive discipline knowing that it is for our good that we might share in his holiness (Heb 12:7,10).

7

Stoning False Prophets

When some people first hear of someone being called a prophet, they might think of a man with wild hair and fiery eyes crying out against sin and calling fire down from heaven. Others think of someone pronouncing judgement and doom, or predicting the end of the world. Though the image may be a little distorted, this is the picture many people have in their minds of prophets as they appear in the Old Testament. The character of New Testament prophets and prophecy is, however, somewhat different. Some people have difficulty with the idea of modern-day prophets and prophecy because they are looking at them through Old Testament spectacles and with an Old Testament understanding. We live in a new era and our relationship with God is under the New Covenant. All this calls for a rethinking of our concept of New Covenant prophetic ministry.

In Old Testament times there were usually only a few prophets in the whole earth at any one time. At times there would be prophets who were contemporaries (Haggai and Zechariah, or Isaiah and Jeremiah), but for the most part they operated in isolation as a lone mouthpiece of God. Often they were not incorporated into the daily religious life and traditions, but stood apart, separated unto God. No prophet symbolises this more than Elijah who stood alone against King Ahab, the prophets of Baal and the sins of a rebellious people. John the Baptist fits that mould as well—the man of God coming from the wilderness to proclaim repentance because of the imminent day of the Lord. In their understanding, the day of the Lord was a day of judgement that would signify the end of the present evil age, usher in the Davidic Messiah and inaugurate the eschatological kingdom of God. Most of the people in Judea came to think of John as a prophet in the Old Testament sense.

These prophets spoke with a clear and unmistakable 'Thus saith the Lord!'. The authority of God's prophets was not limited to the general content or just the main ideas of their message. Rather, they claimed repeatedly that their *very words* were the words which God had given them to deliver: 'I will be with your mouth and teach you what you shall say' (Ex 4:12); 'Behold, I have put My words in your mouth' (Jer 1:9); 'And Balaam said to Balak, "Look, I have come to you! Now, have I any power at all to say anything? The word that God puts in my mouth, that I must speak" ' (Num 22:38).

We do not find in the Old Testament any instance where the prophecy of someone who is acknowledged to be a true prophet is evaluated or discerned so that the good might be sorted from the bad, the accurate from the inaccurate. Because God was thought to be the speaker of all that a prophet spoke in his name, it was unthinkable that a true prophet should deliver some oracle which was a mixture of accurate and inaccurate information. There was no middle ground. They were either true prophets who spoke the very word of God and should be obeyed as such, or they were false prophets and should be put to death.[1]

---

[1] Wayne Grudem, *The Gift of Prophecy* (Eastbourne: Kingsway Publications, 1988), pp. 20–22.

In the Old Testament prophets were frequently representatives of the Lord in the presence of kings—those who had the power to punish them. There was never a question about accurately discerning the genuine word from God. For the prophet, it was only a matter of whether he had the courage to deliver it. The essence of Old Testament prophetic ministry was a chosen vessel delivering what he had received as *direct revelation*. They didn't struggle in their attempt to discern the still small voice or sort out the subtle impressions from their own thoughts. The message was clear and unmistakable. Can you imagine Noah saying, 'I feel the Lord is impressing upon my heart that he's going to destroy the world with a flood and that I should consider building an ark'? Stepping out in faith for them was not a matter of proclaiming with confidence what they only remotely sensed. It was repeating what God clearly said, regardless of the consequences.

Prophecy in the New Testament has a different character. There are not merely one or two prophets for a nation, but the gift of prophecy, the prophetic ministry and the word of the Lord are diffused and distributed throughout the entire body of Christ. I believe there are people with prophetic giftings resident in most cities of the earth where the church is being established. They may be immature, but they are probably present.

Under the New Covenant we don't usually see prophets who live by themselves in the wilderness. The prophetic ministry is a vital part of the greater body of Christ. Prophetic ministers are validated by their involvement in and with the local church, not by their separateness. The church is evangelistic with its evangelists, caring with its pastors, serving with its deacons and prophetic with its prophets. Prophetic ministers serve within the church to help it fulfil its function. They are one of the joints that supply (Eph 4:16) the church, enabling it to be the prophetic voice in the earth. But just because we have called and ordained evangelists, pastors and deacons doesn't mean every believer cannot share the gospel, care for others and serve the church and the world. In the same way, the prophetic word can be manifested through any believer, not just those called by God as prophets.

In the New Testament, the prophetic ministry is directed less at the national leaders and more to the church. In the Old Testament, prophets spoke much of the time (though not always) of judgement. Prophecy today is primarily for edification, exhortation and comfort (1 Cor 14:3).

Although New Testament prophecy does at times come by way of dreams, visions and the audible voice of God, much prophetic revelation can be more subtle. More common forms of revelation are impressions by the Holy Spirit—the 'still small voice' so to speak—as opposed to the always unmistakable audible voice of God.

New Testament prophecy is different because we have a New Covenant, one in which the Holy Spirit dwells in each believer; one in which God has designed for the full expression of his purpose to be revealed through the local church. Though the office of the prophet in the Old Testament existed in a higher realm in many ways, the New Testament gift of prophecy is a better gift based on a better covenant because all can prophesy (1 Cor 14:31). The 'lone ranger' is rare because the Holy Spirit brings the whole body into the process of gaining and receiving the prophetic word.

There is another major difference between New and Old Testament prophets. Because Old Testament prophets received direct and unmistakable revelation, they were 100% accurate. They did not need to have the others discern the prophetic word (1 Cor 14:29). The only way they missed it was because they blatantly changed what God had said or deliberately made up a false prophecy. Consequently, the Old Testament judgement on false prophets was to stone them to death.

'I will raise up for them a Prophet like you [Moses] from among their brethren, and will put My words in His mouth, and He shall speak to them all that I command Him. And it shall be that whoever will not hear My words, which He speaks in My name, I will require it of him. But the prophet who presumes to speak a word in My name, which I have not commanded him to speak, or who speaks in the name of other gods, that prophet shall die.' And if you say in your heart, 'How shall we know the word which the Lord has not spoken?'—when a prophet speaks in the name of the Lord, if the thing does not happen or come to pass, that is the thing which the Lord has not spoken; the prophet has spoken it presumptuously; you shall not be afraid of him (Deut 18:18–22).

In the New Testament, instead of stoning prophets when they make mistakes, the leaders are instructed to 'let two or three prophets speak, and let the others judge' (1 Cor 14:29). The Revised Standard Version translates the passage: 'Let the others weigh what is said.' Paul gives similar instructions to the church in Thessalonica: 'Do not quench the Spirit. Do not despise prophecies. Test all things; hold fast what is good' (1 Thess 5:19–21).

You don't stone people if they miss it once; neither do you believe everything they say if they are accurate 51% or 99% of the time. This idea of prophetic people with subtle impressions of the Holy Spirit making mistakes some of the time is difficult for many conservative Evangelicals. The reason, of course, is that they have failed to understand the transition in prophetic ministry. While they clearly see other aspects of the Old Testament changing under the New Covenant, their understanding of prophetic ministry is still based on an Old Testament model.

Priests and prophets under the New Covenant

The first individual referred to in the Bible as a priest was Melchizedek. He was 'the priest of God Most High' (Gen

14:18). Following the Exodus from Egypt, God instituted a priesthood after the order of Aaron. Until that time, all references to priests referred to those of other ancient religions, primarily the priest of the occultic religion in Egypt. One of Joseph's wives was the daughter of the priest of On (Gen 46:20). So the office and ministry of the priesthood was a well-established religious tradition long before God's instructions to Moses on Mount Sinai.

Three months after being miraculously delivered from Egypt, the Children of Israel arrived at Mount Sinai. Through Moses God declared his intentions to them: 'Now therefore, if you will indeed obey My voice and keep My covenant, then you shall be a special treasure to Me above all people; for all the earth is Mine. And you shall be to Me a *kingdom of priests* and a holy nation' (Ex 19:5–6).

The people were instructed to prepare for the day when God would speak in such a way that each one of them would hear his voice. The people sanctified themselves and gathered at the foot of the mountain on the third day. That morning the thunder and lightning began, and a thick cloud descended upon the mountain. When the Lord descended upon Sinai in fire, the smoke went up like the smoke of a furnace and the mountain quaked. Heavenly trumpets began to blow and continued for a long time, growing louder and louder. Apparently, all the people heard the voice of God as he proclaimed to them the Ten Commandments. Here is how the people then responded: 'Now all the people witnessed the thunderings, the lightning flashes, the sound of the trumpet, and the mountain smoking; and when the people saw it, they trembled and stood afar off. Then they said to Moses, "You speak with us, and we will hear; but let not God speak with us, lest we die" '(Ex 20:18–19).

That is the last time God spoke in an audible voice to the people as a whole. From that time on he used prophets and priests as mediators between himself and the chosen people.

But it was clearly God's purpose from the beginning that the Children of Israel would eventually function as a kingdom of priests; a kingdom in which every person had direct access to God in the hearing of God's voice.

God's purpose for his people, that they should be a kingdom of priests, was fulfilled in the New Covenant. In his first epistle, Peter called the saints a holy and a royal priesthood (1 Pet 2:5, 9). John wrote to the seven churches: '[Jesus] has made us kings and priests to His God and Father' (Rev 1:5). In his vision, John also heard these words in the new song sung by the four living creatures: '[You] have made us kings and priests to our God; and we shall reign on the earth' (Rev 5:10).

In the New Covenant, we are priests because the veil has been removed, and we each have direct access to God, to the throne of grace (Heb 4:16). We need no man or priest to intercede for us, for Christ himself is our constant mediator (1 Tim 2:5). In the same way, we do not need to have someone seek God for us in the way that Saul asked the prophet Samuel to enquire of God on his behalf. In the New Covenant, we can do that ourselves. Jeremiah prophesied about a New Covenant in which each person had the ability to hear from God through the indwelling Holy Spirit:

> Behold, the days are coming, says the Lord, when I will make a new covenant with the house of Israel. . .not according to the covenant that I made with their fathers. . .I will put My law in their minds, and write it on their hearts. . .No more shall every man teach his neighbor, and every man his brother, saying, 'Know the Lord,' for they all shall know Me, from the least of them to the greatest of them, says the Lord (Jer 31:31–34).

In the Old Covenant priestly and prophetic ministries, (a) the calling was reserved for a select few, (b) the requirements were clear and unmistakably defined (ie, the priest's duties were spelled out in detail and the prophets received direct revelation), and (c) the judgement upon them was severe. Prophets were stoned (Jer 23) and the priest died in the presence of the Lord if the sacrifice was unacceptable (Lev 10:1–3).

The New Covenant is different. The emphasis of Peter's sermon in Acts 2 was that sons and daughters, old men and young men, menservants and maidservants—they were *all* going to prophesy in this New Covenant because of the outpouring of the Spirit. Instead of a limited few, everyone is a priest and the gift of prophecy is diffused through the entire body. Instead of the direct audible voice of God revelation, much prophetic ministry is imparted by impressions of the Holy Spirit upon our own hearts. Instead of stoning prophets, we are instructed to judge and discern that which they speak to know if it is from God.

In the generations that followed its beginning, part of the church seemed to have reverted to the Old Testament understanding of the priesthood. This not only robbed an essential truth of the gospel from the church, but it empowered the priests to the extent that the power and privilege of their elevated position became to some a corrupting influence. Early in the sixteenth century Martin Luther, an Augustinian monk and a priest, was troubled by the current understanding of the priesthood. The priests were few and exclusive, the requirements were structured and ritualistic and the judgement was severe on them for failure.

Luther began to teach a doctrine that we know today as the 'priesthood of the believer'. This New Testament understanding of priesthood is an accepted foundation of evangelical theology, but in his day it was radical enough to get him condemned to death. Luther also taught the doctrine of 'private judgement', ie, every person can hear God and interpret the Scriptures for himself. That was another radical idea for the sixteenth century, but it is the beginning place for the New Testament understanding of prophetic ministry. Every Christian can hear from God, can discern and be led by the Holy Spirit. Ministry that was exclusive in the Old Testament (prophet and priest) is now diffused and common in the New.

From one perspective, the New Testament doctrine of the priesthood of all believers and private judgement (or hearing God for oneself) certainly complicates things. In fact, it can be downright messy. The human fallout from Luther's emphasis on these doctrines has caused innumerable arguments, denominational splits and even wars. To some, it would seem simpler and neater if we had a hierarchy of priests and a single person who spoke for God. But God's plan all along has been to have a kingdom of priests and a prophetic church made up of his very own sons and daughters.

Though it can sometimes be messy, unpredictable and hard to control, no Evangelical is going to deny the doctrine of the priesthood of all believers. All of us agree that this would be an issue worth defending. New Testament prophetic ministry is an extension of the idea that we can all hear from God (Luther's private judgement). However, prophetic ministry in the church is extremely difficult for some fundamentalists and conservative Evangelicals, simply because they embrace an Old Testament understanding of the prophetic in which only a few receive direct revelation that is 100% accurate—otherwise they are stoned.

Packaging prophetic ministry

For the most part, the same type of New Testament prophetic gift can operate in very different packages. Usually people have no problem with the lady in the prayer group who feels a burden to pray for someone, who senses the Holy Spirit leading her prayer, and who states that God is 'impressing' something on her heart. All of this is in a package that most people are familiar with and understand. But if she speaks up during the Sunday morning service in her non-charismatic church and loudly proclaims her revelation interspersed with 'thus saith the Lord', she could get a significantly different response. Here we have the same words and the same message, but delivered in a very different package. Sometimes I think some of us are too concerned about the package and not concerned enough about the message, although I realise that if you want your message received then you must send it in a way that will appeal to your audience.

It bothers me when a prophetic person prefaces everything with 'thus saith the Lord'. Part of the reason for this is that they may have heard others do it. Perhaps it is an attempt to be more dramatic or to increase the chance of being heard. Sometimes it may be because they have an Old Testament understanding of the prophetic. Whatever the case, I think it is important that we encourage people to do without the drama and mysticism when they proclaim that God has spoken. Because there are many levels of personal revelation in the New Testament church (from slight impressions to audible voices to angelic visitations), the messenger needs to be clear about what he or she has received. Slight impressions don't need to be punctuated in the same way as an open vision. You may eventually find yourself sounding like the boy who cried 'Wolf!' when you say, 'But I *did* hear something this time. Thus saith the Lord *really*!' And all the people yawned.

Many prophetic ministers I know act on prophetic revelation by making suggestions or asking questions of the person being ministered to. For example, if you feel impressed by the Spirit that a person you meet has a particular illness that God wants to heal, you can simply ask them if they have the problem. The gifts of the Spirit can operate in the course of natural dialogue. We don't have to roll our eyes back, speak in King James English and end with 'saith the Lord'. Tone it down. It will still work!

I think that sometimes there is a personal motivation that is involved with a person's reluctance to do away with the Old Testament prophetic tone. Some people may be too interested in 'hitting a home run'. They want to deeply impress their audience. They fail to understand that God gives them revelation through Holy Spirit impressions, not so they can be known as a prophet, but in order to help other people. Even if you ask the person about their illness because of revelation from the Holy Spirit, if they acknowledge it, there is then the temptation to add the comment: 'Well, the Lord told me that.' Sometimes we want to establish that we were responsible for hearing the word rather than just letting God do his will in their lives.

Prophetic revelation in the New Testament is often based on impressions given by the Holy Spirit that have to be properly discerned. Therefore, we have to reel in the Old Testament ministry style to reflect the more subtle nature of New Testament revelation. There's not as much personal glory with that more subdued style, but we don't stone prophetic people who make mistakes either. Prophetic people need to understand that this is not about personal recognition and glory. The gift is diffused throughout the body of Christ in order that he alone will be uplifted.

Corrupting power of the prophetic

If you could raise the dead on only one out of ten attempts, you could gather a crowd of 100,000 people anywhere in the world in twenty-four hours' notice. If you could raise ten out of ten, you could rule and control any nation on earth. Remember they tried to make Jesus king because he healed the sick and multiplied the fish and the loaves. The release of any type of supernatural ministry with overt demonstrations of power puts a lot of attention on the people God uses. Because genuine miracle ministry is so unique, the millionaires and kings will come to serve such anointed vessels. There are a lot of millionaires in the world, but how many people can hear from God like the prophet Elijah? A prophet of the stature similar to those in the Old Testament would face incredible temptations and pressures. William Branham's prophetic ministry in the 1940s and 1950s was so unique that he came to be revered by some on a level with the Old Testament prophets Elijah and Elisha. Regretfully, some of his followers referred to him as Elijah. Branham died in 1965, yet there is still a group of churches that are known as his followers, who gather on Sundays to hear his teaching tapes from the 1950s. Branham himself, wanting to be a teacher, ended up promoting certain heresies. His ministry stands for ever as a warning for prophetic people to submit to the local church and its teaching ministries. A lone ranger prophet is susceptible to many heresies, just like a lone ranger evangelist, pastor or teacher.

Contemporary prophetic ministry without corruption

Paul Cain also has a prophetic stature similar to an Old Testament prophet. Paul met William Branham on several occasions. I think Paul only saw Branham minister in person one or two times. They never had the chance to become friends. Paul heard of the doctrinal errors that developed in Branham's ministry at the end of his life, but never had enough first-hand information to know exactly what Branham believed.

Paul Cain has had the opportunity to meet with two United States presidents and several heads of state in Europe and the Middle East to declare God's word to them because of his prophetic gift. I believe this will become increasingly common as God raises up more prophetic people like Paul who receive clear discernment into the secrets of people's hearts, as well as clarity about future events. This type of prophetic ministry attracts the attention of people from all walks of life, including the presidents and kings of nations.

Generally, the gift of the prophetic in the New Testament is dispersed throughout the body of believers. However, there are people whom God raises up with special giftings. Though the anointing on such people may appear to be like that of an Old Testament prophet--that is, having direct and unquestionable revelation—both they and the people who hear them must remember that they are New Testament prophets. They are subject to error, to correction, and are subject to the body of Christ. They are not to be lone voices in the wilderness, but a gift to the body serving to further the ministry of the church.

8

God's Strategy of Silence

There are tremendous pressures that weigh upon people who are called to prophetic ministry. Whether their prominence is a result of God's promotion or man's, the pressures increase with their prominence. And it doesn't take a very high success rate to gain a huge following. If a prophetic person who regularly prayed for AIDS patients and paraplegics saw only one out of ten healed, he or she could fill the largest stadia in the world, with people longing to hear their words, see a miracle and, perhaps, even touch their garment. Any kind of regular supernatural manifestations and giftings must be accompanied by a great measure of spiritual maturity, or the pressures will become a stumbling-block surely to be tripped over.

One of the more difficult things to deal with as a prophetic minister is coming face to face with people in great need, only to find that God is completely silent on the matter. God's heart and mind may have previously been revealed to them with great clarity and astounding detail concerning a dozen other people in the same congregation. Then when confronted with a person in a desperate situation, who obviously has more need for a word from God than anyone, the same prophetic minister may sense nothing from the Holy Spirit—complete silence.

This awkward situation, which will inevitably arise, presents a real test of character and maturity for the prophetic person. If he or she says, 'I have no word for you,' people will be disappointed, if not angry, at the response. The person's ministry reputation may be on the line. If he or she is in the prophetic ministry full time, future invitations and honorariums may be affected. People's faith in them will be diminished since they only give prophetic words occasionally. The pressures of people's expectations and assumptions push many prophetic ministers into dangerous waters that can eventually shipwreck their integrity as well as their ministry.

The great temptation is to give a word you don't have in order to release the pressure of the moment. It is the same temptation that provokes the teacher to answer a question using information of which he is not certain. The teacher desperately hopes no one listening realises that he's way beyond what he actually knows. For many teachers, it's just too hard to say, 'I don't know.' The same immaturity and pride that cause the teacher to think his credibility is based on his ability to know it all prevent the prophetic minister from saying in a despairing situation, in which his or her reputation is on the line, 'I have no word for you.'

Notwithstanding the pressure of people's expectations or his own desire to help a person in need, a prophetic minister must discipline himself to remain silent when God is silent.

Manufacturing a word in our own mind, whether it is out of compassion or the pressure of our ministry credibility, can work directly against the purpose of God in the life of a church or an individual. It is a lack of integrity that never builds people's faith in the long run, even though the people may be excited for the moment over a man-made prophetic word.

Sometimes people add to what God says because they are trying to be 'more loving than God' by quickly answering people's questioning hearts and giving them a word even when

God is silent. It is giving in to the temptation to add a filler. Though this can cause some significant problems, it is not what I consider false prophecy or a false prophet. Jeremiah 23 contains the Lord's condemnation of those who had been prophesying out of their own imagination, who 'speak a vision of their own heart, not from the mouth of the Lord' (23:16). The pronouncement of judgement on these false prophets is frightening indeed. Consequently, it really bothers me when this passage is used to criticise prophetic people who don't discern the voice of the Lord accurately or who give in to pressure to embellish the word out of their own heart and mind. The condemnations of Jeremiah 23 are directed at prophets who deliberately changed the specific pronouncement of the judgement God gave to them for Israel's national rebellion. And they knew it. They disregarded God's warning to the nation and fabricated a prophecy proclaiming only wonderful things and assured the Jewish people that God would protect their nation from judgement. This is the context of Jeremiah's dirge against the false prophets. This is quite different from a situation where an immature prophetic person erroneously prophesies out of his own heart of compassion for a person in need.

God never said to kill prophetic people who make this type of mistake. The threat of death was to the type of prophet who opposed God's discipline on an entire rebellious nation. My point is that the context of Jeremiah 23 is not primarily directed as a warning to sincere young prophetic people who are new and unskilled in prophetic ministry.

People are constantly thrust into ordeals in which they agonise over the question: 'Why would God allow a certain person to continue in suffering?' In order to 'bail out' God and his reputation, some pastors, teachers or prophetic ministers rush to provide the answer. Maturity as it relates to prophetic ministry is not only the willingness to speak a difficult word, but the willingness also to be totally silent, even when offering a 'prophetic word' might seem so appropriate.

The temptation to manufacture a word is the same for the individual receiving as it is for the prophetic minister, only from a slightly different perspective. Some people find the circumstances they are in so acute that they absolutely *must* receive a word from God, and they must have it *immediately*. Their situation may be desperate, or it may be that they are just weary of waiting for God to answer. In either case, there are times when there is no word from God; there are no confirming circumstances that suggest an answer from God; and even the famous prophet who gave almost everyone else a word says he has received nothing from God for them. Having spent all their perseverance waiting for God, they manufacture a word for themselves and then take off with it.

The impatient King Saul, tarrying for the prophet Samuel who seemed to be in no particular hurry, is a prime example of this. King Saul had gathered the people at Gilgal to fight against the Philistines, but Samuel delayed in arriving to offer the sacrifice. Seeing that after seven days of indecision and inaction his army was beginning to desert, Saul could wait for the prophet no longer. A full-scale national crisis was at hand. He went ahead and broke God's law by offering the sacrifice himself, even though Samuel had specifically warned Saul to wait for him to do it. Of course, as soon as he had finished, Samuel showed up. 'The Philistines were ready to attack me at Gilgal,' said Saul, 'and the sacrifice was not yet made to God. Therefore I felt compelled, and offered the sacrifice myself' (see 1 Sam 13:12). Samuel, who was long overdue (at least by Saul's watch), offered no apology, but chastised Saul for his foolishness in disobeying God by failing to wait on God's prophet to come in God's timing. 'The Lord would have established your kingdom over Israel forever,' Samuel told him, 'but now your kingdom shall not continue' (1 Sam 13:13–14). It was a serious sin against God's law for a king to offer the sacrifice—a job strictly reserved for the prophet and priest. Saul refused to wait on God in a time of personal crisis. He went on without God, resulting in a far greater crisis.

God's silence or inactivity at a time when *we* desperately want God to act or speak reveals the spiritual maturity of both the people and the prophet. This was Saul's first major test after becoming king, the first of many that he would fail. In the same way the delay of Moses revealed the golden calf that was 'hiding in the hearts' of the Children of Israel. On the other hand, disillusioning questions about God's lack of intervention and what seems to be God's inattention, caused King David to agonise and pour out his soul in the writing of the Psalms. In the instance of the golden calf, waiting revealed the inclination to idolatry in the people, and in David's case, waiting revealed that his heart was truly after God.

Each believer must go through the struggle of learning to walk with God when he is silent. It is an inescapable part of spiritual growth, and it is imperative that a prophetic minister understand God's strategy of silence. As one who supposedly speaks for God, if a prophetic minister doesn't understand that God does not always speak, even in the most desperate of situations, he will inevitably manufacture words for people when God's specific purpose is for him to say nothing. Regardless of your well-intentioned efforts to make God look good, you become a stumbling-block for those whom you seek to help.

Walking confidently in darkness

Part of the process of spiritual maturity is being brought to the edge of our understanding and then walking on ahead without understanding what will happen next. Like Peter, God sometimes calls us to walk on water, which is to proceed with a certain amount of uncertainty. Isaiah 50 describes such a person who fears the Lord: 'Who among you fears the Lord? Who obeys the voice of His Servant? Who walks in darkness and has no light? Let him trust in the name of the Lord and rely upon his God' (Is 50:10).

Walking in darkness as it is used here doesn't refer to moral darkness that comes from sin or demonic oppression. It simply means walking in unknown territory without clear light and reassuring direction. Isaiah continues in the next verse: 'Look, all you who kindle a fire, who encircle yourselves with sparks: Walk in the light of your fire and in the sparks you have kindled—This you shall have from My hand: You shall lie down in torment' (Is 50:11).

This verse highlights the peril and torment of those who refuse to wait for God's light, and create their own fire in an attempt to manufacture some light. The fire speaks of fleshly activity. This man-made counterfeit fire can never substitute for God's light. Such people who resort to this counterfeit will lie down in turmoil instead of lying down in safety of peace. This is a warning not to manufacture prophetic words!

Isaiah warns the person who fears the Lord not to kindle their own flame. Do not manufacture an artificial light out of your frustration with the darkness and, as it relates to the prophetic ministry, do not manufacture the light for someone else. God's silence forces us to grow in our confidence in him as a Person as we walk through the darkness by lacking a sense of direction. We then realise that he was very near all along. In this way, we develop our own personal history with God.

In my years of relating to prophetic people, I have observed that this is one of the major ways in which God tests and refines them. This challenge could be called 'learning the art of dangling'. I have seen many people struggle with this divine dealing over the last number of years. It seems as though God holds out to the last possible moment to observe if we will panic or trust him in our times of uncertainty.

Misunderstood silence

God's personality is infinite in its complexity and creativity. We think of God being perfect in every way. God has a 'divine personality', perfect in his wisdom, love and goodness. His dealing with each of us is in terms of building a relationship of love. But more often than not our monolithic misunderstanding of how God *should* act in a given circumstance causes his action to seem contrary to our way of thinking. One of the things we should learn from the Gospels is that often Jesus did not answer people in the way we think God should. At times when we think he should answer, he is silent. At times when we suppose he should intervene, he is inactive. If for no other reason than that, prophetic ministers should be careful not to presume what God should say or do in any given situation.

As he passed through the region of Tyre and Sidon, Jesus was confronted by a Syro-Phoenician woman who was crying out, 'Have mercy on me, O Lord, Son of David!' As desperate as she was to see her demon-possessed daughter set free, Jesus seemingly ignored her and did not initially answer a word. As she continued to cry out, he seemingly refused her saying, 'I was not sent except to the lost sheep of the house of Israel.' Still pursuing him, Jesus seemingly insulted her: 'It is not good to take the children's bread and throw it to the little dogs.' Not to be denied, the woman would not turn away. Jesus finally rewarded her and said, 'O woman, great is your faith! Let it be to you as you desire' (Mt 15:21–28).

We would have been astounded had we witnessed this encounter. Jesus' seeming lack of response, lack of action and even his apparently rude behaviour certainly does not fit within the model of how we believe the God of love should or will act. But from our perspective today, it is obvious that Jesus was probing, testing and drawing out her faith.

Because of our preconceived notions, we often draw wrong

conclusions from God's silence or his apparent lack of inter-vention on our behalf. Most commonly, we conclude that God's love for us has waned or that we are unworthy of his attention or perhaps that we are being punished for something. But that was certainly not the case with Lazarus. The Scriptures say sev-eral times that Jesus loved Lazarus, along with his two sisters, Mary and Martha, but his delay in coming to help Lazarus in his greatest need was precisely calculated: 'Now Jesus loved Martha and her sister and Lazarus. So, when He heard that he was sick, He stayed two more days in the place where He was' (Jn 11:5–6).

We know that Jesus' seeming lack of response had nothing to do with lack of love, but was to fulfil the redemptive purpose of God. The ensuing miracle was a prophetic sign to many of his own resurrection. But for Lazarus, Martha and Mary it taught them something more, namely, to trust God always, even when it meant walking in darkness beyond the edge of their under-standing.

From prison John the Baptist sent his disciples to enquire of Jesus. After sending them back to John, Jesus commented, 'Assuredly, I say to you, among those born of women there has not risen one greater than John the Baptist' (Mt 11:11). John was the greatest, but Jesus did nothing to prevent him from being beheaded by King Herod. Jesus' inaction was neither from a lack of love for John nor a lack of worthiness in John himself.

People stumble over the fact that God doesn't speak or act in the way we think he should. But from Isaiah 50 we learn not to manufacture our own light when we walk in darkness. From Saul we learn not to run ahead of God when the answer is delayed. From the Gospels we learn that God's silence does not mean we are rejected or unloved, but must be understood in the light of God's redemptive purposes.

There are those 'Why, God?' questions that are a normal part of the walk of faith for all of us until the very end. For those who have allowed the Holy Spirit to perform his work in their lives, the 'Why, God?' questions are accompanied by a growing peace and trust rather than disillusionment and unbelief. God wants us to learn to be at peace in our souls by virtue of our relationship with him, not by virtue of the information about our circumstances that we sometimes receive from him. People searching for God's peace and comfort are more commonly looking for it by asking God for information about their future. He wants our peace to come first by addressing any problems in our personal relationship with him. A prophetic person must understand that often what people desperately want is the prophetic word that God himself refuses to give. They ask for information about circumstances, and God gives information about their relationship with him. They want peace and assurance, but have a different formula for it. If God is not answering, sometimes we are asking the wrong questions.

A famine of the word of the Lord

There can be a variety of reasons known only to God for his silence or for the times he withholds the sense of his presence. His purpose for this can be to teach us faith, to train us in his wisdom or even to bring judgement for those who have deliberately rejected his words to them. Amos declared the following to Israel:

> 'Behold, the days are coming,' says the Lord God, 'that I will send a famine on the land, not a famine of bread, nor a thirst for water, but of hearing the words of the Lord. They shall wander from sea to sea, and from north to east; they shall run to and fro, seeking the word of the Lord, but shall not find it' (Amos 8:11–12).

It seems strange to us that God would withhold his word from Israel, who seemed to be searching so hard to find it. What actually happened was that Israel had consciously ignored and rejected God's word already spoken to them through the prophets. They wanted very much for God to speak, but didn't want to hear what God wanted to say. So they sought hard to hear him say something else.

What happened to Israel as a nation takes place in the lives of stubborn individuals. Sometimes in a counselling session every possible solution that can be offered is met with the reply, 'I've already tried that,' or, 'I already know that.' You find yourself under pressure to come up with some exotic answer which they have never heard and have never tried. The reason that the wisdom and word of the Lord are not clear to either of you is that the answer to the problem is sometimes the most fundamental one and the first one you thought of. For example, to a man who has been greatly hurt and offended, God's specific word to him is that he should fully forgive. But having refused and rejected that simple but challenging answer, he begins a long process of running to and fro seeking the answer to his growing problem. Even though he is apparently seeking diligently, the famine of the word of the Lord is because he deliberately rejected what God had already said clearly. It was simply too unpleasant for him to receive.

Whether God's silence or inaction is a part of the normal maturing process or a judgement from the Lord is not always clear, but it is certainly not indiscernible. God's silence as divine judgement comes as a result of conscious rebellion against the clear conviction of the Holy Spirit. Although mankind's heart is deceitful and desperately wicked, unless you are in the last stages of reprobation, you can usually know the sincerity or the resistance of your own heart to the Holy Spirit. Though in our own hearts we try to rationalise our way out of things, usually deep down inside we know the reality of our insincerity or a specific issue with which God has been dealing.

The more elusive problem is for those who are sincere

(though immature), yet are deceived by the powers of darkness into thinking that the silence of God is a sure sign of his displeasure and abandonment.

Be silent with revealed knowledge

One vital test of a prophet is in his or her willingness to speak a hard word from God, and then to accept the resulting reproach and persecution that are the normal burden of prophetic ministry. It is a test of surrender and consecration to God.

Then there is another vital test of remaining silent when God has not spoken, regardless of the apparent need of the moment. This is a test of honesty and integrity before God.

A third vital test is the willingness to remain silent about what God has clearly revealed to you. This is a test of maturity and security in God. Some prophets want to ensure that they are always credited for having received revelation from God. Children who know a secret just can't stand it. They've got to tell someone. Just because God divinely opens your eyes to a certain revelation doesn't necessarily mean you are supposed to share it. I think some of the prophetic words that people submit for the entire church are actually not meant to go beyond themselves.

Caution with corrective words

We also encourage prophetic people, especially if they are new in this ministry, to be very careful in delivering directional or correctional prophecies. This category of prophecy obviously has the potential of causing more pain and confusion than any other kind. If someone does receive what they believe is a direction or a correction for someone else, I would recommend the following steps:

1. Share the 'revelation' with a more mature prophetic leader for his or her counsel without necessarily revealing the identity

or identities of the people in question.

2. Pray for the people and their situation and ask God to give you insight on the right time to share it.

3. If you deliver it to them, do so in a non-authoritative style so that they can have an easy way out and don't have to reject you if they can't receive the message. If it is a true word and their heart is right before God, it will make its impact even if you share it in a non-authoritative 'thus saith the Lord' style. Also, the principles of Matthew 18 and Galatians 6 must be carefully followed when it comes to correcting someone who is in sin, even if their sin has been revealed through the operation of prophecy.

The difficulty of symbolic prophecies

Interpreting a prophetic word can be difficult because of the highly symbolic word pictures that are often involved. People who are immature in the prophetic ministry may also need to restrain themselves for a period of time from sharing their insight in order to watch to see how their word comes to pass. This will help them learn how to interpret and apply what they are receiving. They may first have to learn the ABCs of how prophecy functions and how on-the-job training can be effective. This is one reason why recording prophetic words is important. Many times a prophecy or spiritual dream can make an impact on someone after the scenario has already been played out if it has been recorded and dated in a prophetic person's diary.

It takes a mature and seasoned prophetic minister to be silent when God is silent, and then at times to be silent when God has shared something that is for their ears only.

9

Origins of the Prophetic Call

I frequently use the term 'prophetic minister' instead of the term 'prophet'. It's not that I think it is always wrong to refer to someone as a prophet. However, it would be wise to do so cautiously and sparingly. There are great differences among people's prophetic giftings, as well as their levels of experience, maturity and credibility. Consequently, we have felt it necessary to define our terminology to distinguish somewhat the different levels and types of prophetic callings and anointings.

We have four categories we use to define prophetically gifted people in our church. We will discuss these four categories throughout this chapter.

Contemporary prophetic ministry gifts

My friend, Wayne Grudem, PhD, a professor at Trinity Evangelical Divinity School, has written one of the best books on prophecy that I've ever come across. *The Gift of Prophecy* should be studied by all serious students of the prophetic ministry.

One of the major stumbling-blocks many people first face when investigating the validity of prophecy is the question of its authority. If prophecy is some kind of 'divine utterance', why does it often sound so pitifully weak? Why aren't we recording the people speaking 'the word of the Lord' and including it in our Bibles?

Grudem does an excellent job of answering these questions. He explains that the Old Testament prophets were called and commissioned to speak 'God's very words', which carried an absolute, divine authority. In the New Testament, he argues that only the apostles had that same authority to speak and write 'God's very words'. All other prophecy is simply 'speaking merely human words to report something God brings to mind'. What this accomplishes for Grudem is a helpful distinction between the divinely authoritative 'very word of God' that became our Scriptures, and the words of New Testament prophets which must be sifted (1 Cor 14:29) and were at times neglected (1 Cor 14:30). He argues convincingly for a qualitative difference between the 'very words of God' spoken only by those with apostolic authority (ie, New Testament Scripture) and the inspired messages of the prophets in the New Testament.

Of course, while Paul and the other writers of the New Testament did at times write 'God's very words', it must be acknowledged that they did not always speak 'God's very words'. While personally affirming the divine inspiration and infallibility of Scripture, I believe that Paul could have written additional letters which were not necessarily 'God's very words'.

Can it work the other way round? Can people today speak 'God's very words' occasionally, even though they can't write Scripture? Is all prophecy, as Grudem argues, only 'human words reporting something God brings to mind' and therefore a mixed up combination of divine inspiration in the human spirit? While affirming the value of the 'mixed lot', we may if we are not careful argue ourselves into a position where God's word can never come through with clarity and fidelity.

Thus we can make a clear distinction between the authority of Scripture and prophetic utterances. Yet it does not seem to me impossible that a person may speak a prophetic word or words that are accurate in every detail and as such are God's words. In saying this, I do not mean to suggest that any contemporary prophetic word should be treated in the way in which we treat Scripture. *Everything* must be tested. However, I do believe that some individuals may be peculiarly gifted in the prophetic and may on occasion be judged to speak with great accuracy.

As Wayne Grudem states, in most cases, prophecy is reporting 'in human words what God brings to mind'. God conveys to our mind thoughts which we communicate in contemporary language. They are a mixture of God's words and man's words. Some 'prophetic words' may be 10% God's words and 90% man's words, while others have a greater revelatory content.

Nevertheless, I have found that those who move with a remarkable degree of accuracy in the prophetic do so by receiving revelation from God by means that go beyond the 'reporting in human words what God brings to mind'. On occasion God speaks to his servants in an audible voice. Additionally, open visions of the spiritual realm and/or visions of future events are modes of communication that are familiar to those who move in the prophetic realm with a remarkable degree of accuracy.

This helps to explain why some prophetic utterances 'ring true' more than others. I have attempted to graph this phenomenon of mixing our thoughts and ideas with God's words:

God's words		
		Man's words
Strong prophetic	Average prophetic word (mature)	Weak prophetic word (immature)

What I am trying to illustrate is that while it is possible to speak 100% accurate words from God, most often prophecy is a mixture. Sometimes this yields a 'mature' word that reflects ideally what God would like to communicate, and sometimes his word is communicated in a much less than ideal fashion, yielding a 'weak' word of lesser value, but still not to be despised.

Whatever the case, and however good or reputable the prophet or prophecy may be, we are called to weigh what is said (1 Cor 14:29–30), including of course those rare occasions when an audible voice is heard 'from heaven' as it were, and Paul encourages the Thessalonian church: 'Do not despise prophecies. Test all things; hold fast what is good' (1 Thess 5:20–21). If the prophetic utterance is from God, then the Holy Spirit will bring the words home to our hearts and give us an internal witness of the fact that it is indeed something God is saying to us.

Who can prophesy?

The church, from its very inception on the Day of Pentecost, was to be of a prophetic nature. It would appear that the gift of prophecy is available to all (Acts 2:14–18), and Paul urges the Corinthians to seek this gift (1 Cor 14:1, 39), while acknowledging that not all are prophets (1 Cor 12:29). What is going on?

Again, I find Grudem helpful, but not adequate. His definition of prophecy as 'speaking merely human words to report something God brings to mind' allows for a type of prophetic utterance that is possible for every believer. Rightfully so. He also acknowledges that in the New Testament some people ministered more regularly in prophecy and were called 'prophets' (eg Agabus, Philip's daughters, Barnabas). He does not, however, acknowledge that there was an 'office' of prophet, something Pentecostals and charismatics have argued over for years. He argues that 'prophet' is more a functional description than an office or title. The key would be

> greater and lesser degrees of prophetic ability, ranged all along a wide spectrum, in any given congregation. Prophets would differ in ability among themselves, and would also see changes in the extent of their own prophetic abilities over a period of time. Those with a high degree of prophetic ability would prophesy more frequently, at greater length, with more clear and forceful revelations, about more important subjects, and over a wider range of topics (pp. 208–209).

What Grudem has pointed out is that some people, like Agabus in the book of Acts, ministered regularly in prophecy, and that while we may not want to give him the 'office' of 'prophet', he had an acknowledged and reputable ministry in prophecy.

I would like to expand on this idea of a continuum and suggest four levels of prophetic ministry.

Level I—Simple prophecy

Any believer who speaks something God has brought to mind. This is usually within the 1 Corinthians 14:3 scope of encouragement, comfort and exhortation that doesn't include correction, new direction or predictive elements of prophetic words.

Level II—Prophetic gifting

Believers who regularly receive impressions, dreams, visions or other types of revelation. These are usually very symbolic, being in the form of parables and riddles. This group receives more regular prophetic information than the first group, yet substantially lacks clarity in understanding what it receives.

Level III—Prophetic ministry

Believers whose gifting has been recognised, nurtured and commissioned for regular ministry in the local church. There is still a strong parabolic element in what they receive, but through the process of team ministry, it is possible to discern much of the interpretation and application of their revelation.

Level IV—The office of the prophet

Believers whose ministry is somewhat like the prophets of the Old Testament. They often minister in signs and wonders and are judged at times to speak accurate words from God. This doesn't mean they are infallible, but rather their words are to be taken more seriously than others' words. Their credibility is clearly established by their long proven track record of accurate prophecies.

The following chart will hopefully illustrate the relationship between these four levels of prophetic ministry and the person's ability to speak God's words with high fidelity.

| IV Prophetic office | III Prophetic ministry | II Prophetic gifting | I Simple prophetic |

I have personally met many people at levels I and II and these groups account for the vast majority of those who prophesy in charismatic-type churches.

Conclusions and summary

What I have attempted to do is show that there is a type of prophetic ministry in the church today in which men and women may at times prophesy with phenomenal accuracy.

While these words may or may not be mixed with the prophets' own words, I believe we should acknowledge that mature and gifted people can speak God's words.

I have also attempted to clarify the issue regarding who can prophesy. What I have described as different levels of prophetic ministry (I–IV) is simply an attempt to provide labels for what most authors who have written on prophetic ministry believe. What I have called 'Level IV—the office of the prophet' represents a maturity and power in prophetic ministry that parallels the Old Testament ministries of men like Samuel and Elijah.

There are really no clear-cut standards for deciding if a person is at Level I, II, III or IV or exactly what the distinctions truly are. These are not biblical distinctions. These are simply categories that help us to communicate with each other more effectively. It may become apparent that more levels are necessary, but I believe that the initial groupings of I–IV will provide some framework for further research.

Our church, Metro Vineyard Fellowship, has had a few Level III prophetic ministers through the years and they occasionally minister together with Level II gifted people in the regular activities in the church and at special conferences. These conferences sometimes provide the emerging Level II gifted ministers with opportunities to minister side by side with the Level III prophetic ministry.

We initially had hoped to develop a training strategy for emerging Level II and III prophetic ministries, but I now feel this should wait until more understanding on specific roles and functions in the church today is compiled.

The sovereign gifting and call, the intense processing that leads to brokenness before God and the discharging of the prophetic ministry, seem to be the essential ingredients of development in prophetic ministry.

For too long, much of the church has not valued prophetic ministry. It is my hope that this book will encourage further study of this important subject. The current emphasis in many circles on 'signs and wonders' has caused some to begin to accept the validity of contemporary prophecy and, for them, Grudem's book will prove to be a useful tool. However, books will not accomplish what the Lord is now doing. I feel that our generation is going to be significantly impacted by many Level III prophetic ministries throughout the land and more than a few Level IV prophets. Pastors will need to learn how to effectively nurture these prophetic ministries and incorporate them into the ministering life of the church. I firmly believe that the church will yet become the prophetic community which Peter described in Acts 2.

I know hundreds who are in the first category, that is 'simple prophecy', and there are many people in the second category, in which the believer is used periodically to give a strong prophetic word. There are maybe twenty to twenty-five people whom I know personally or have heard of who have a proven prophetic ministry as described by Level III. These are men and women who regularly receive dreams, visions and supernatural encounters as a part of their lifestyle. They function in this way as a gift to the body of Christ. Many of these people may one day be recognised as being in the office of a New Testament prophet. In my mind, recognising a person as a New Testament prophet (in the office of a prophet by our terminology) involves three issues:

1. There is a certain level of *supernatural giftedness* that is evidenced by regularly receiving divine information from the Holy Spirit. The validity of this gift is proved over time and is not an issue of having just one prophetic word, regardless of how accurate or spectacular it seems.

2. There is *godly character* that is an essential mark of a true prophet. Jesus said that you would know true and false prophets by their fruit. The fruit I believe Jesus is referring to in this passage includes the Holy Spirit's presence and sanctifying work

in the person's life. There is a brokenness, a kindness, a self-lessness and a compassion that have the mark of the Holy Spirit on them. These are people who diligently seek to cultivate holi-ness and deep passion for Jesus in their lives. Also, fruit of prophetic ministry obviously includes the kind of impact that it has made on others.

3. Then there is the *matured wisdom* of God that has come through experience and relationship with the Holy Spirit. This wisdom enables the person to be an instrument of the prophetic knowledge and power of God in a way that builds up the people of God and the purpose of God. This wisdom is foundational to using the prophetic in a manner that will build up the local church.

I have seen the Holy Spirit work in these three areas with the prophetic ministers I know. Some of them have grown in these areas more than others. Nevertheless, I am reluctant to refer to people publicly as being in the office of a New Testament prophet. Paul Cain is an example of someone whom I would consider a Level IV prophet. I suppose there may be many with that kind of calling, but I personally know only a very few at the present time who could be spoken of as in the office of a prophet when measured by the maturity level of their gifting, character and wisdom.

I'm not at all comfortable with labelling most people who prophesy as prophets. I would rather err on the side of caution. I tend first to put the prophetically gifted person in a lower cat-egory until they are well proved in the context of long-term relationships in the local church. I think the church does itself harm when it allows people to identify themselves quickly as 'apostle' or 'prophet' simply because they consider themselves to be so or because it looks good on a brochure. By doing so, we trivialise the gifts and callings of God and hinder the emerg-ing of God's genuine ministry gifts to the church.

Sovereign calling

Being called into some kind of prophetic ministry is not necessarily the reward of how diligent you have been to seek to mature in that gift. It's not even determined by how eager you are to grow in wisdom and character. It is a matter of God's sovereign call. The same thing is true with regard to each individual manifestation of the Spirit. Paul writes to the Corinthians: 'But one and the same Spirit works all these things, distributing to each one individually *as He wills*' (1 Cor 12:11).

We serve a personal God who has his own purposes for each individual. God is not an impersonal force. A Tibetan monk may go through the exercises and disciplines thinking he will become an ascended master. But the gifts and callings of God are not primarily based on our striving, seeking or searching, but are based on his sovereign choice and by his grace. It is not a matter of our efforts to attain or develop spiritual skills. It is all about God's sovereign calling and God's gracious giftings.

People often ask us in conferences how they can grow in the prophetic and receive more words from God. Paul Cain usually says, 'We can only teach you what to do with the words. Nobody can teach you how to receive words from God. Those things are the activity of the Holy Spirit in our human experience. We can only teach you how to co-operate with the activity of the Spirit, not how to produce the activity of the Spirit.'

I wasn't sure what would happen when John Wimber asked me to pray for the gift of prophecy to be imparted to people at the 1989 Vineyard Conference in Anaheim. I suppose there were many people who wanted me to pray for them to be called to the office of a prophet. Of course, there is no way I could do that. It is God's choice. However, we have seen people who were prayed for in such conference settings suddenly begin regularly to receive an increase from the Spirit of the Lord in the area of dreams, visions and prophetic words. Many of them have continued to experience an increase of prophetic gifting from that time on. To some extent, this kind of gifting is transferable, but only to the degree that God sovereignly ordains. I believe that there was already some measure of the calling of God to the prophetic in these people's lives.

The catalyst that releases or activates the gift of God in a person is sometimes a divine encounter at salvation, or even years later by a sovereign visitation of God without any human agency. Sometimes it happens suddenly in childhood or it may happen after the person has been a Christian for many years. With some it is a slow growth of the prophetic anointing, while with others the gift is imparted through the laying-on of hands (1 Tim 4:14; 2 Tim 1:6).

There is a place for diligently seeking to grow in gifting, character and maturity. But while diligence causes you to grow within your calling, it does not determine your calling.

Origin of the call

There are numerous ways people are called into the various types of prophetic ministry. I want to share some things I have observed concerning the origins of the prophetic call. I want to say at the beginning that the people I refer to are merely some of those who have either fellowshipped with us or have been a part of our team. It is by no means an attempt to provide a comprehensive list of the *premier prophets* of the land. And there are many prophetic groups and prophetic ministers around the world that I don't know much about. It is, however, easiest for me to talk about the ones I know.

Called in their youth

Paul Cain is an example of being called to the prophetic ministry while still in the womb. The prophet Jeremiah and John the Baptist were called in the same way. Paul's mother, Anna

Cain, was forty-five years old and very sick when in 1929 she became pregnant with her first son. She had three terminal illnesses. She had serious heart problems, large cancerous tumours in her breasts and uterus, besides being terminally ill with tuberculosis. Anna had been sent home to Garland, Texas from Baylor University Hospital to die. There was nothing the doctors could do for her. But like Hannah she promised to dedicate the child in her womb to the Lord, that is if she lived long enough to deliver the baby (1 Sam 1:11). As it was, the tumours in her womb would prevent the child from coming through the birth canal. Late one evening as she was desperately crying out in prayer, the Lord spoke to her through the appearance of an angel. In essence, he promised that she would not die and that the child would be prophetically anointed as a minister of the gospel. Anna was healed immediately and lived sixty-five more years until she had her 105th birthday. She nursed her baby on the very breasts that had been so riddled with cancer.

Anna Cain never talked to Paul about the Lord's call upon his life. She wanted the Lord himself to reveal this directly to him. This happened one night when Paul was eight years old. Paul was in his bedroom. Suddenly, the angel of the Lord appeared to him and spoke clearly to him about his sovereign call. This is when Paul began to be used prophetically. God spoke very powerfully to Paul and called him to this type of ministry. The voice of the Lord was also heard by Paul's sister who was present in the room. She became a life-long prayer warrior on behalf of Paul and his ministry.

Immediately after this experience, the gifts of prophetic revelation began to operate in Paul's life, ie supernatural words of wisdom and knowledge and the discerning of spirits (1 Cor 12:7–10). He also developed a passion for the Lord and a burning desire to preach. At nine years old, Paul used to set up discarded railway spikes in rows, pretending they were people sitting in pews, and he would preach to them. Paul also found that he 'knew by the Spirit' things that were going to happen, as well as information about people's personal lives. Paul's Baptist pastor, Dr Parish, would take him along on some of his pastoral visits during the late 1930s and early 1940s. The young boy would sometimes know by the revelatory gifts of the Spirit which of the sick people were going to be healed. Many times this knowledge came to him in the form of a vision.

For example on one occasion, while en route to a hospital, Paul related to Dr Parish that he had seen a vision of a lady who was in bed dying of cancer. She was approximately sixty years old and was wearing a rose-coloured dressing gown. Standing at the foot of her bed would be her brother, Tom, dressed in his work clothes. When they arrived at the hospital, they found the scene exactly as Paul had described. Paul hadn't previously known anything about this lady or her brother. They prayed for the lady and she was completely healed.

At the age of nine, Paul began preaching to his young friends. He first gathered a crowd of a dozen children from the neighbourhood, along with his grandmother and his parents. They all sang praises to God and then Paul preached. Public preaching by a boy of that age was something Paul's Baptist church found hard to handle. When Paul was about eighteen the Pentecostals began inviting Paul to preach at their evangelistic meetings. They seemed to have less objection to boy preachers.

By the time Paul was twenty, he had a regular radio ministry and was conducting healing services in a small tent. He began travelling across America ministering as an evangelist who emphasised physical healing. Those were the early days of the healing movement which swept through the pentecostal churches during the 1940s and 1950s. Paul began to discover that he was resented and even rejected by some of the movement's leaders. This was partly due to his youthfulness, but also because Paul had not yet gained the maturity and discretion necessary to function in such a powerful ministry.

The origin of Paul Cain's calling was from his mother's womb when the angelic messenger visited her. It was later confirmed to Paul by the Lord himself at the age of eight. It had nothing to do with his personal diligence or his own righteousness. The calling was by God's sovereign grace, and the prophetic gifts immediately began to operate in Paul's life after the angel of the Lord had appeared to him.

John Paul Jackson is a prophetic minister who was on the pastoral staff of Metro Vineyard Fellowship for about five years and then with John Wimber and the Vineyard Christian Fellowship in Anaheim for another three years. Like Anna Cain, John Paul's mother also had an experience with the Lord indicating that her son would one day have a prophetic ministry. John Paul was converted at an early age and began immediately to move in the gifts of the Spirit. However, he went through a period in which he did not follow the Lord fully. His heart had grown cold. During that time the revelation gifts ceased. In his late twenties, when he recommitted his life to Christ, the manifestations of the Spirit returned in a very strong way. He currently pastors a church in Dallas, Texas, and he continues to travel as God uses him in the prophetic ministry.

Bob Jones, whom I have already mentioned in this book, is a man who has had a very profound prophetic ministry. His former lifestyle was that of a thief, a brawler, a bootlegger and an alcoholic. Bob had very little religious background and did not become a Christian until he was in his late thirties. Nevertheless, Bob had several angelic visitations and supernatural experiences as a boy which indicated that he would have a prophetic ministry in his adult life.

When Bob was thirteen he heard an audible voice from heaven call his name. When he was fifteen he saw himself in a vision being brought before the throne of God. This experience terrified Bob. It took him several months to get over the vision. It never occurred to him until after his conversion that these things represented God's call on his life rather than God's judgement.

Immediately after his conversion, to Bob's amazement, the prophetic gifts began to operate powerfully in his life. Bob is another example of how the gifts of grace and the calling of God were given as a result of God's grace, not our striving.

Stirring up the gift

Michael Sullivant is an excellent pastor and teacher who for many years believed in the prophetic ministry. Yet Michael is a person, like myself, whose function in the church would be described as mostly in the areas of leadership and teaching. But several prophetic people told Michael that they sensed that he would have a prophetic ministry one day. That seemed unlikely since there was no notable sign in him of any prophetic gifting or calling.

In May of 1990, Paul Cain singled him out at one of the meetings in our church. He spoke to Michael about a prophetic calling and encouraged him to set aside time to seek the Lord and to let the Lord remove some dross from his life.

Michael retreated to a cabin in Colorado for thirty days. Beginning the very first night and for thirty nights in a row, he had prophetic dreams. Since that time, Michael has grown rapidly in the prophetic ministry.

John Wimber was a professor at Fuller Theological Seminary who began to teach on healing. Soon after he started to teach on the subject, healings began to take place. Before long the word of knowledge began to operate in a mighty way. For John Wimber there was no dramatic angelic visitation or voice from heaven. He simply began to step out in faith in whatever way seemed appropriate for him. In the process, the gifts of the

Spirit began to operate through him. The manifestations of the Spirit working through him enabled him to recognise, in retrospect, that God had certainly called him to his particular type of Holy Spirit ministry.

The calling of God on your life is a function of his divine plan, issued before you ever lifted a finger to serve him. It doesn't matter if you haven't had a special divine visitation. God, nevertheless, has gifts and callings designed for your life. Bible training, discipline, fasting and praying will not change your calling. However, these spiritual disciplines *will* enhance the release of the calling that has already been divinely determined. The goal is not to try to get God to call you as a prophet or to endow you with spiritual gifts. It is a matter of stirring up the gifts and callings already determined for you by God.

The pain of the prophetic calling

There is always a temptation to want something before we understand it. Then once we've got it and understand the difficulties associated with it, the temptation is to want to get rid of it. There is a lot of misunderstanding about prophetic ministry. Spectators don't realise how little the prophetic people understand about what is happening with their own lives and ministries. If a person has a desire to be involved with prophetic ministry, it should not be because it seems exciting. The pain, the perplexities and the attacks upon these people are far greater than anybody knows. Some of the prophetic people I know have spent times in their ministry with painful complaints, asking the Lord to lift the prophetic call off them. The glory that appears in a conference setting is so untypical of their everyday lifestyle.

We encourage people to find their joy in loving God, knowing that God loves them and in being a faithful servant. They should not think that some spectacular ministry will make their life happy. I have never met a prophetic person yet whose life was significantly made happy because of his or her gift. Typically, they have experienced demonic attack, opposition from godly people and great perplexity in their own soul. They may see so much, but they often can't understand the full meaning of what they see.

Prophetic ministers seem to have more disappointment with God than the average person. They often see clearly how things should be or how God plans for them to be. But they have to wait in faith for a longer time because they have seen further ahead. They are much more prone to the Proverbs 13:12 difficulty: 'Hope deferred makes the heart sick.' Because their expectations are typically higher, they are typically more deeply disappointed.

It's easier for other people to enjoy life as it is because they are not so burdened with how things are supposed to be, and they don't have to live in the pain of it all the time. Jonah had a big disappointment with God. So did Jeremiah, who complained that the Lord had tricked him. Every time he opened his mouth he got into trouble. He was perplexed, he was ridiculed and he wanted to give up. Nevertheless, the word of the Lord was like a fire burning within him and he could not hold back the word (Jer 20:7–10). Some of that pain comes with the calling. Other difficulties are sometimes leadership-induced, as in our case, because we as a church didn't know how to nurture and administrate prophetic ministry.

An important reality check

Let me offer a general encouragement to all of us. Through my years of being personally involved in the lives of fellow believers, I have observed a common hidden agenda that often operates within their lives. This motivation is driving many of them, but it is subtle and very hard to pin down. I would call it a commitment to avoid pain and suffering at almost any cost. Even as committed Christians, we are tempted to invent theologies, and work long and hard trying to create a painless environment for ourselves. We will use the Bible, other people and even spiritual gifts and power to seek to achieve this end. In fact, I have found that many people gravitate to seeking out various forms of prophetic ministry for this reason. They imagine that if they could more clearly discern the voice of God, then he would surely lead them into a problem-free and totally satisfying life on earth. The problem is that when God speaks, he sometimes tells us to believe and do things that ultimately lead us into more testings, perplexities and pain! Some of the most confusing and spiritually dry experiences and seasons come upon prophetic people directly on the heels of being used by the Holy Spirit. Often they cry out for God to use them, and when he does, they complain about 'feeling used'!

> But in all things we commend ourselves as ministers of God: in much patience, in tribulations, in needs, in distresses, in stripes, in imprisonments, in tumults, in labors, in sleeplessness, in fastings; by purity, by knowledge, by longsuffering, by kindness, by the Holy Spirit, by sincere love, by the word of truth, by the power of God, by the armor of righteousness on the right hand and on the left, by honor and dishonor, by evil report and good report; as deceivers, and yet true; as unknown, and yet well known; as dying, and behold we live; as chastened, and yet not killed; as sorrowful, yet always rejoicing; as poor, yet making many rich; as having nothing, and yet possessing all things (2 Cor 6:4–10).

The above scripture describes three categories of experience that are characteristic of genuine apostolic Christianity and the very seal of authentic Christian leadership. I call them the negative pressures (vv. 4–5), the positive qualities (vv. 6–7) and the divine paradoxes (vv. 8–10) of life in Christ. If we are in true fellowship with the Father and seek to live according to his word, then all of these things will come our way in different measures from season to season. We should expect these opposing and perplexing experiences to show up in our lives. If we are reconciled to this reality from the outset, then we are able to respond redemptively to them as they occur.

I believe in praying for the blessings of God to come our way and I would never encourage anyone to go looking for trials or sufferings. We really don't have to. They will automatically come just by our living in a fallen world. God intends to use the pain of these things to draw us into a relationship of mature faith and fervent dependency upon him. Pain and passion are inseparably linked. If there's no pain, there'll be minimal passion for God and minimal compassion for others. Pain causes us to reach fervently to Jesus and to rejoice passionately when God answers us in the midst of our pain. And even when we enter into intimacy with God by the Holy Spirit (which the prophetic ministry is given to enhance), it will not be totally satisfying to our hungry souls. The Scripture teaches us that we are destined to live with a certain groan for more of God in our souls. Paul refers to this lack of perfect satisfaction in Romans 8:22–23: 'For we know that the whole creation groans and labors with birth pangs together until now. Not only that . . . even we ourselves groan within ourselves, eagerly waiting for the adoption, the redemption of our body.'

The gift of the Holy Spirit is a down payment of the full inheritance that will be ours to enjoy fully in the age to come. Even full-blown end-time revival is not heaven on earth — read the book of Revelation! I find many people spending their spiritual, emotional, physical and relational energies seeking ways to escape all the pain of this 'groan' within ourselves. Our deepest satisfaction and the perfection of all things is certainly promised, but its fullness is delayed until heaven. We can know some significant victory, joy and satisfaction in this age. But only in part. First Corinthians 13:12 teaches us that in this age we only know and see in part. Our victory and satisfaction are not yet in fullness. But in the age to come we will see him face to face and our victory, joy and satisfaction will be in total fullness. We are called to wait joyfully and patiently for it as we love God and others in this evil age.

I certainly don't want to discourage anyone from becoming as intimate with God as they can and there are thrilling, glorious and pleasurable experiences with him to be had. But as deep and precious as they are to our hearts, they are less than the deepest satisfaction and pleasure we will know when we see him face to face. The groaning for God's fullness and our longing for heaven are vital for a healthy Christian life and to the salvation process in which we are engaged. A healthy Christian life is characterised by genuine joy in the midst of groaning for God's fullness, which will only be fully satisfied when we see him face to face in heaven. Thus, even the greatest prophetic ministry with unprecedented power will not satisfy our deepest groan for God's fullness. We must never forget this truth.

10

Pastors and Prophets: Getting Along in the Kingdom

The prophetic ministry in the local church functions in an 'orderly freedom' only when both the pastors and the congregation have a common understanding of how things should work. It is worth mentioning at this point one aspect of our public worship services. Throughout the week or during the worship service there are usually many people who have had some kind of prophetic dream, vision or impression. Many feel they have a word from the Lord that relates to the life of the church or to that particular worship service. Nevertheless, we very seldom have spontaneous prophecies voiced from the congregation. Neither do we usually have a pause for prophetic words after three good worship songs. It is important for unity and peace that the church understands how the prophetic ministry functions. So the principles of nurturing and administrating prophetic ministry need to be understood not only by pastors and prophets, but by the majority of the congregation as well. One of the reasons I wrote this book was because of the need to have a unified systematic teaching on the prophetic available to our church body. We've had new people join our church over the last few years who have not understood basic principles. It doesn't seem edifying to repeat these principles continually to the church because then the body becomes too focused on the prophetic. My hope therefore is that this book will clarify basic principles so that we can work within a common framework of understanding.

Non-prophet leadership

Some people are surprised that I can be the pastor and overseer of prophetic people without being prophetically gifted myself. This misunderstanding has recurred numerous times. Often as a guest speaker I have been encouraged by the pastor to 'take my liberty'. By that they meant I should feel free to single out people in the congregation and give them personal prophetic words from the Lord. When I tell them I don't usually prophesy over people, they often think I am just trying to be falsely humble. On several occasions I've had to insist, 'Listen guys, I'm not joking. I am not a prophet.' Some pastors are surprised by this, and some are disappointed. They were hoping to see a spectacular manifestation of God's power when I preached at their churches.

I have had private conversations with many wonderful pastors who were frustrated because they were not able to move in spiritual gifts as freely as some of the people in their congregation. Often some of these prophetic-type people in the church are spiritually immature in other ways. The pastor feels insecure and thinks they are apparently more 'in tune with the Spirit'. Consequently he feels too intimidated to correct such prophetically gifted people.

As much as the prophetic ministry has found expression at Metro Vineyard in Kansas City, I seldom prophesy, and even then there is no 'thus saith the Lord' tagged on for emphasis. If I have something I feel is from the Lord, it will usually come out in my preaching and teaching without my mentioning it as a prophetic word. While some feel pressure to sound more spiritual because of their leadership position, I am careful to tone down any appearance of prophetic gifts because of my position as senior pastor of the church.

When pastors realise that I am a pastor/teacher with very limited prophetic giftings, their response is often something like this: 'I never realised you could have this kind of thing happening in your church and survive as a pastor without being a prophetic person yourself.' It doesn't take a prophet to nurture and administrate prophetic ministries in your church. It takes a leader with a vision for a multi-gifted, diverse team.

Pastor as prophet: The fox in the hen house

A pastor with a strong gifting in the prophetic or the miraculous needs to understand the dynamics of his role. Those giftings, if not used with wisdom and restraint, can have a negative effect on his ability to pastor the church effectively. I run into some pastors who want to create a mystique about their gifting in order to perpetuate the image that they live on a higher plane. Perhaps the intention is to inspire people in the church to press on to spiritual maturity. Often the secret motivation, however, is to enhance people's confidence in the pastor's spiritual and pastoral leadership. A pastor needs to understand that if he falls into this trap of showing off his own prophetic giftings, it will hurt and hinder the whole church in several ways. In the end, some people lose trust in the pastor's wisdom and leadership abilities if the pastor too often makes his case by saying that God told him to do it. Some will feel unable to relate to him on his level of exalted spirituality. A pastor can also end up with people wrongly attached to him as a prophetic leader instead of them being attached to the Lord. This is evident when too many people want to be with him, hear from him and get a word from him. The insecure pastor enjoys this attention for a couple of years, but he will eventually burn out. Pastors wanting to lead primarily through prophesying are making a serious mistake in their leadership style which will have a demobilising effect on the church. As the senior pastor, only rarely can I give a 'thus saith the Lord' kind of direction, warning or correction. The people will become weary of such terminology attached to the directions of the pastor if it comes too often.

A pastor in one city began regularly to experience the gift of prophecy. He saw his prophetic ministry as an extension of his pastoral ministry. Consequently, he used little restraint. His role as pastor was used as a platform for his prophesying. The fox was in the hen house in the sense that there was not much pastoral restraint to his revelatory gifts. As time went on his role as pastor began to be overshadowed by his role as prophet. He was calling out people and giving them words in most services. He began to struggle and was soon prefacing most of his prophetic words with 'thus saith the Lord', many of which did not come to pass. Nevertheless, he was beginning to demand the clout of one with a proven prophetic office. It wasn't long before everything in the church began to break down. The people were devastated, the church was a wreck and, finally, after a couple of years, the doors were closed.

Pastors and teachers serve a different purpose from that of prophets and evangelists, who have predominantly power gift ministries. Most who try to emphasise both equally come under additional pressures. God wants all the gifts to rest in a body of people, not just in one or two leaders. One person functioning as both the head prophet and senior pastor can present a conflict of interest similar to that which would have existed in the Old Testament if a single individual were to hold the office of both high priest and king. It was forbidden within the Jewish nation for one person to serve both governmental and priestly functions, one reason perhaps being the inherent conflict of interest. I'm not saying at all that it is unbiblical to be both the strongest prophetically gifted person and the senior pastor. I am saying that it is rare and the situation would have added pressures.

There is a fresh wind of the Holy Spirit blowing all across the world today. With each new outpouring of the Spirit comes unusual and unexpected manifestations. This current moving of the Spirit is only a beginning of the kind of deluge prophesied for the end times. The church desperately needs wise and mature pastors and teachers who can lead, nurture and administrate prophetic people in the midst of such a supernatural downpour, or the wineskins will burst and the new wine will be lost. Michael is one example of a person who is called to the rare position of being both prophetic and a pastor/teacher. Consequently, he plays a unique and essential role in the nurturing and administration of the prophetic ministry at Metro Vineyard. Michael's ministry effectively enables the new wine to flow and increase without bursting our wineskin.

There are usually people in a church who are sensitive to prophetic ministry. They seem aware of exactly how much 'freedom of the Spirit' they felt in the last church service. They often bemoan the fact that the pastor is not more prophetic. Actually, a God-ordained pastor is equipped with the leadership gifting God wants him to have. He is in a strategic position to help the church succeed in becoming more prophetic if he wisely uses his gift of leadership. More often striving, insecure pastors, rejected, pushy prophetic people and the lack of a diversified team ministry are factors that hinder the flow of power and revelation through the church. If everyone was a prophet, the church would function like a runaway train without an engineer.

The pay is the same

We all have to learn to be secure in what God has called us to be and realise the value and importance of each person. Paul, in his letter to the Ephesians, was explaining the different gifts and callings in the church when he wrote: '. . . the whole body, being fitted and held together by that which every joint supplies, according to the proper working of each individual part, causes the growth of the body for the building up of itself in love' (Eph 4:16, NASB).

Satan is a master of sowing into people's hearts discontentment about who they are and what God has called them to do. This is a problem throughout the whole body of Christ. People are always leaning over the fence, longing for the other cow's grass. I have met numerous prophetic people who want to be teachers. They clearly see all the pain associated with their prophetic gift, and they imagine that the teacher has only success, respect and a life of appreciation. Many teachers I know who have seen genuine prophetic people want to prophesy.

Paul pointed out in his letter to the Corinthians that one part of the problem is *inferiority,* 'because I am not an eye, I am not of the body' (1 Cor 12:16), and the other part of the problem is *superiority,* 'the eye cannot say to the hand, "I have no need of you" ' (v. 21). We have created a lot of this by attaching status to different ministries and giftings. Prophets are ultra-spiritual, apostles are to be super-ultra-spiritual, pastors and teachers a little less, and so on down the line to deacons, ushers and the person who prints the newsletters. A lot of this is magnified by Western culture. The social status associated with different functions in the body of Christ causes people to do rather eccentric and unbalanced things, and in the end it affects the way the members of the body do their part to supply what is needed. We have often said at our church, 'Whether you are raising the dead or taking a nap, if you are doing God's will, in the end the pay is the same.'

At Metro Vineyard in Kansas City we are related to several prophetic people of international stature. Some have lived in Kansas City and others have been related by friendship. We also relate to about a dozen people who have full-time travelling prophetic ministries and many people who regularly have prophetic dreams, visions and so on. A pastor like myself in this situation needs to be secure in his limited calling. I am at peace within my limited spiritual giftings. Actually, that was not a big problem for me. I could see the terrible difficulties and pressures people like Paul Cain and others had experienced as a result of their prophetic ministry. I didn't covet that for a second.

One of my main callings is in the area of intercession. For years I have found grace to cry out for a revival of passionate Christianity across our nation. I was content within those limited spiritual boundaries before I had ever heard of any contemporary prophetic people. That was a real key for me, and I still identify with my intercessory burden and calling. My first book, entitled *Passion for Jesus*, was a clear expression of my heart and primary life message. I am still not a prophetic minister and I probably never will be to any great degree. I am neither an exceptionally good pastor nor a particularly effective manager. Primarily, I exhort and encourage people and I also lead a team of people who have gifts that are very different from mine. Their gifts are stronger than mine in many diverse areas. I love it.

One of the most important lessons I had to learn was that I did not have to be intimidated by people who heard directly from God much more frequently and much more dramatically than I did. At first I was terribly reluctant. I was a pastor in my late twenties, relating to people like Bob Jones who received profound and accurate prophetic words. It can be intimidating. My reluctance to confront prophetic people came to a head at nearly the two-year mark of the prophetic ministry in our church.

'Duelling Prophets Sunday'

During the second year of pastoring our new church plant in Kansas City, I had sat and watched five or six prophetic people regularly compete for the microphone during the Sunday morning services. I was starting to get exasperated because it was becoming clear to me that there was a lot of hype in what had been going on for the last few months. Some of the people were growing tired of feeling manipulated by these prophetic people and were starting to voice their feelings. On one Sunday morning in December 1984, two of the main prophetic people got into a 'prophetic duel' right in front of the church. One stood up and proclaimed something to this effect: 'Thus saith the Lord, "A great thing is going to happen."' Then the second man stood up and said, 'Thus saith the Lord, "Better things are going to happen." ' Then the first prophetic guy topped him. Not to be out-prophesied, the second man answered back by giving something even better. They went about three rounds each.

I was sitting in the front row getting really angry. It was clear to me what was going on. These two guys were yielding to a common temptation among prophetic people and were competing against each other to be the top prophet of the church. It was scandalous, embarrassing and ridiculous, and everybody could see it except these two prophetic men. A dozen people came up to me afterwards and asked how much longer I was going to let this go on. Usually I tried to cover for the prophetic people by encouraging folk to be patient and reminding them of all the great things that had happened through them. But this time the men concerned had crossed the line. The emperor—or rather the prophets—had no clothes, and the only ones who didn't know it were these two prophetic men themselves.

Another leader and I got both of these prophetic men together and had what turned out to be a very strong and direct confrontation. Both of them were defensive, and threatened that if I didn't accept their ministry style and what they had to say, the Holy Spirit's blessing would leave our church. I was really surprised they would resort to such fleshly means of manipulation, because previously they had given prophetic words about the future that had already come to pass exactly as they had predicted. But when they issued this warning (to let them do what they wanted or the Holy Spirit would leave), it pushed a button in me. My eyes opened, and, at that point, I saw the rank carnality in all of it.

Normally I would have been intimidated by people who had previously prophesied with such dramatic accuracy. But I was provoked and offended, so I rose up and told them both to leave. I essentially informed them, 'I am finished with you two!' That was such a disillusioning time for me that I was tempted to do away with all of the prophetic ministry, the miracles, the supernatural confirmations—everything, and we would no longer have prophetic ministry in our church.

I'm glad now that I didn't give in to my anger and frustration because of the marvellous things that I've seen God do in our church through the prophetic ministry. But there was one very positive thing that came out of what we call 'Duelling Prophets Sunday'. Something broke inside me, and from that point on I was no longer afraid to confront prophetic ministers, even if they had previously had authority to call fire down from heaven.

Both of the prophetic ministers told me that they were finished with this church, and they assured me that God was cancelling all the tremendous prophetic words spoken over the church. They assumed that God was going to leave with them. It sounds silly to me now, but there was a time when I would have thought that God's blessing would leave if these men's feelings were hurt and they left. But God doesn't abandon you because a prophetic minister feels offended. He can be used mightily and effectively by the Holy Spirit, but he is not the mediator between us and God. Only Jesus is.

These two men went out from our meeting to complain against me to some of the key people in the church. But these people called me and congratulated me, saying, 'Thank you, thank you, thank you!' That's when it dawned on me that it was *not* the prophets who had the gifting and calling of governmental leadership in our church. I also realised that if leaders don't stand up and speak the pastoral wisdom God has given them, prophetic people would not only destroy the church, they would destroy their own ministries as well. Much of what happened on 'Duelling Prophets Sunday' was my fault, because I had not exercised my leadership gift and responsibility. I had allowed these men to get themselves into a difficult and embarrassing situation. I realised that the team of governmentally gifted people in our church had a lot more pastoral wisdom than the prophetic men did about church life and how people respond to the word of God. In one short week, the way I viewed my own ministry and that of our pastoral leadership team totally changed.

Within two weeks both of those prophetic men had come back and repented to me of their ambition and carnal motivations. This put a new confidence in me that some of those deep uneasy feelings I had had about their ministry style were really wisdom and discernment. I determined that I was no longer going to dismiss or quench those feelings. Since that encounter, I have decided that whenever I have a nervous feeling about what the prophetic people are doing, I am not going to ignore it. To neglect the responsibility to lead the prophetically gifted people will usually result in harm to the church and to the prophetic ministers.

The motivation of rejected prophets

Most prophetic people are in touch with their giftings long before they cultivate the corresponding wisdom, humility and character that are necessary to succeed in prophetic ministry. In the beginning, they may appear arrogant or pushy because of their zeal. As years go by, their pushiness usually comes from fear, hurt and rejection. Most prophetic people who have been around for a few years have had their hands slapped many times. Some of them have been dealt with harshly, without proper explanation and without the security of a good relationship with church leadership. By the time I met Bob Jones he had been mistreated by many people and had deep ministry scars. John Paul Jackson was so shell-shocked by negative experiences with previous churches that he was expecting to be totally rejected by us at any time. The average person who has been in the prophetic ministry for ten years is pretty beaten up and bruised. This is especially true if the prophetic gift was active in their early years. By the time they are forty or fifty they are often very guarded and suspicious of authority figures. Those coming into prophetic ministry later in life may also have problems with rejection. These past histories of dysfunctional relationships with leaders in the church cause prophetically gifted people to put a lot of extra pressure into gaining honour and acceptance. Several problems can develop if they give in to those temptations.

Many of the prophetic ministers are looking to build up enough credibility to ensure that they won't be ousted. Many of them just want some security. They feel that if they gain enough clout they won't have to worry so much about being rejected. Everyone knows that you don't cut a great player from your football team just because he is having one bad game. Also, they feel that if they can build a reservoir of credibility, when they have something to say they won't have to fight to be heard. Since building clout is so important to them, there is the temptation to push hard to get credit for having heard accurately from God. I do not think it is always appropriate to acknowledge publicly the person who gave me a key prophetic word as I share it with the church. However, a rejected prophet can hardly resist proclaiming, 'Oh, *I'm* the one who gave him that key prophecy!'

One temptation often leads to another, and when the prophetic person or his or her revelation is not publicly recognised, the temptation is to whisper to the influential people in the church in an attempt to be recognised. Some prophetic people are determined to be heard one way or another. Obviously this does not make for a good friendship with the pastor, who sees all this as selfish ambition and manipulation.

Sometimes prophetic people come into conflict with pastors because they push too hard for their revelations to be spoken at the public church services. If the pastor doesn't give the prophetic minister a public platform in the church, a temptation for the prophetic person is to judge the pastor as having a controlling spirit or to think he is a stiff-necked Pharisee who is always resisting the Spirit of God. Sometimes people with this attitude will gather their prophetic groupies together to pray against the pastor.

All of this (and more) is usually a result of wounded and rejected prophets giving in to former hurts and present temptations. The problem is also amplified by pastoral leadership that does not see beyond the prophetic person's pushiness to discern the fears and hurts that drive them. If prophetic people, who are misunderstood, wounded and rejected, give in to their fears and temptations, they will extend great efforts to obtain credibility and acceptance. But, ironically, it will always backfire on them. The harder they try, the worse it becomes. Sadly many of them have not yet figured this out.

Pastors are usually reluctant to confront a seasoned prophet. Why? Because the pastor has his own insecurities. I was very much aware of my inability to hear from God as they did. I operated on the premiss that if they could receive the divine information, certainly they could hear from God on how to apply it. I made a false assumption.

Insecure pastors and leaders

Knowing where and how to draw the line with prophetic ministry minimises the insecurity and fear that a pastor normally experiences when first encountering such people. If a pastor understands how to deal with these people, he is less afraid of them. Most pastors don't mind if things are a little messy if it is going to be profitable at the end of the day. But if they don't see the long-term benefit, they're going to say, 'Enough of this!' and press the reject button. For the most part, pastors don't want to be embarrassed, and they don't want their people becoming hurt and confused. They are trying to protect their people and keep peace in the church.

Prophetic people often have a very keen sense of being answerable to God. Pastors have that sense too, but they are also very aware of being answerable to people. A pastor probably feels both concerns differently from the prophetic minister. The pastor realises he is answerable to God, but knows that, if there is a problem, on Monday morning he's going to hear it from the elders and from half of the congregation. The pastor also has the conflicts and practical pressures of meeting the budget. And when people get upset, they often leave and disrupt the economics of the church. What that means to the pastor is that he might have to fund part of the ministry staff. The prophets don't usually live in that arena or with those pressures.

Many pastors yield to insecurity and the fear of man. They have seen too many churches fail and so many people hurt by it. They sometimes take their eyes off God and yield to fear when things go beyond the comfort zone. They must learn to lead without fear and yet keep balanced in the area of risk-taking without sacrificing pastoral wisdom.

The pastor and leaders sense several things: what God wants, what the people are going to say, and half a dozen other factors that, if left unattended, may cause the wheels to come off the entire operation. It is good for prophetic people to understand all of this so that they don't see pastors and leaders as people who are simply wanting to quench and oppose the move of God.

Most pastors I know will let unusual, unprogrammed and even some strange looking things happen, as long as they know it is not hype or fake. Pastors are often afraid of things happening beyond what is of the Holy Spirit. They would rather cut things off a little before the danger zone. Prophets are almost always willing to go a little bit further than the danger zone to make sure that we do everything that might be of the Lord. If we do a little bit more, in their way of thinking, it's better than not doing all of it. The prophet's biggest fear is that he might not get everything unloaded that God wants unloaded. The pastor's biggest fear is that he doesn't want to get the church into hype because he has to maintain a long-term relationship with them. Prophets and pastors have the same motivation, being afraid of missing God, but from different points of view.

One of the greatest benefits of having prophetic ministry in the church is that we need the input from proven, gifted people who carry the prophetic burden of God's heart without the same fears and anxieties that often accompany the pastoral leadership team. Many times those fears and anxieties serve as blinders to the pastor. It may be harder for a pastoral leader to recognise a flaw in the church if it has been there a long time. This flaw seems so obvious to the prophetic people. Perhaps the pastor is more acutely aware of all the problems that will arise from trying to fix the problem. On the other hand, a general understanding of pastoral and administrative problems associated with leading the church should enable prophetic people to understand the pastor's dilemma more clearly.

The church's greatest effectiveness is realised when the diverse gifts and personalities work together as one team ministry. But it takes a lot of patience and honouring of one another to deal with the pressures that come with nurturing and leading a church with a variety of giftings. Unless we learn to show honour to each other and the unique work that the Holy Spirit is doing in each person's life, we may end up in a holy war, especially if the gifts and personalities are strong. Without team ministry, none of these gifts would be able to prosper. I believe this is especially true for the prophetic ministry.

11

The Prophetic Word in Public Worship

The way we handle prophetic words in a regular public worship service has evolved over time. For the first two years in Kansas City, we allowed almost everything to happen spontaneously without any of the procedures we have today. During those first years, as well as in the years that followed, there were numerous occasions when a prophetic word was spoken forth by someone in the congregation that resulted in great benefit to our church.

A couple of years into the life of Metro Vineyard, one of the men on our prophetic team got up and said that the Lord had spoken to him very clearly and powerfully. It was 1 February 1985. He said that the Lord was going to provide a building for this body of believers in four months—by 1 June. He went on to say that two men in business suits were going to come up to us and make us an offer we could not refuse.

At that time we had a 700-member congregation and no building. The meetings were held in a school and we had a lot of meetings! Everything we owned had to be packed and unpacked for each meeting. There were numerous inconveniences that made this arrangement tiresome to everyone.

This prophetic minister was telling the congregation what

everyone so desperately wanted to hear: all of this was going to be over in a few months. Everyone clapped and cheered wildly at the word.

I stood next to the man giving the prophecy, feeling complete panic race through my soul. I didn't exactly know what to do. The word was so clear: two men in business suits making an offer so good that we could not refuse it; 1 June; a building we didn't have to look for (and we had been looking long and hard without any success). I was struggling with the idea that a great deal was at stake here. What if I let it go without comment or correction, and it didn't happen? The backlash directed at this guy was going to be minor compared to what the people were going to say to me for letting them be messed around by this prophetic word. This particular minister had a lot of credibility and a fairly accurate track record with regard to some significant prophecies. Nevertheless, he still made mistakes occasionally. All I could think about was all the people who would want to lynch me on 2 June because of their dashed hopes if a building was not provided by God on 1 June. I knew that I only had four months until 1 June. As the pastor, I felt that the prophetic word put me way out on a limb.

The building committee were not very enthusiastic either. In fact, I think they felt a little undermined by what had happened. They had already put in many hours of hard work in looking for a permanent facility. It was not clear to me what to do with this committee. If I believed the prophetic word, the new building committee should be dissolved, and if not, I needed to encourage them to keep working. The truth was that I really didn't believe the word. I felt that the prophetic minister probably had an incorrect interpretation of what God had shown him. Thus, I told the building committee to keep searching.

I informed the prophetic minister afterwards how much I would have appreciated it if he had talked to me before putting me into such a difficult position. The Duelling Prophets Sunday a few months earlier had begun a process of working out a system for administrating the flow of prophetic words in our worship services. We were only in the beginning stages of learning to give pastoral leadership in this area. Believe me, this incident helped move the process along.

The committee continued looking for a building for the next three months. As May rolled around, they had located no facilities that were even considered possibilities. I was really sweating and already preparing my answer to the congregation for the meeting in the school on 2 June. However, on 10 May, two men asked an associate and myself to lunch. The first thing they did was apologise for their dress. They felt overdressed wearing suits and ties (which they rarely did), but they had just come from a special meeting. They went on to say that they had a building to offer us. These businessmen had a burden to reach young people and had bought an indoor soccer field in order to win kids to Christ, but things were not working out as they had hoped.

'We've heard about your ministry,' they said, 'and we want you to have our building. Our soccer schedule is over on 28 May, and we want you to take it immediately so that there will be no vandalism.' So three weeks later, on Saturday, 1 June, we took the keys, started cleaning up and had our first church service there on Sunday, 2 June. It happened just as he had prophesied it—two men in business suits made us an offer we could not refuse and they did it before 1 June. I was overjoyed.

All of this could have happened without any prophetic proclamation in the Sunday morning service. I would much rather have heard the prophetic word in private and hidden it in my heart. It certainly would have been easier on my nerves. But God knew exactly what he was doing. Most of our congregation lived in a semi-affluent area of town. This new facility was ten miles south of where we were currently meeting and it was located in a lower socio-economic area. Most of the church growth experts say that a ten-mile move to a different socio-economic area would be negative for any church, normally resulting in a loss of membership. But the prophetic word was so precise that the church accepted the new location as being from the Lord. Of the 700 people in our church, we lost only about three or four families. God was not only preparing the building, he was also preparing the people for a significant move through a prophetic word that morning.

This building that would seat over 2,000 people was offered to us at such a low price that we were able to pay it off completely in three years. It was truly an offer too good to refuse.

When the prophecy was first given, of course, we did not know how accurate it would eventually prove to be—hence my decision to keep the building committee working away until the word was fulfilled.

'Anything goes' approach to prophetic ministry

Very often people who are new to the prophetic ministry are concerned about the Holy Spirit being quenched. Most of them don't understand the length, height, depth and breadth of God's love and patience with his people. He is not as easily quenched as we imagine, especially with people who are sincerely trying to do his will but seem to get it all wrong. That's the way I started out. I thought of the Holy Spirit as a sensitive, skittish dove that would fly away at the slightest ruffle. He's not that easily offended. The Holy Spirit is very secure, very powerful and very kind.

Consequently, in those first two years, except for the really flaky stuff, I would let almost any type of prophetic utterance go without correction or any attempt to administrate it. In my mind, at that point, attempting to administrate the flow of the prophetic was equal to standing in the way of what the Holy Spirit wanted to do. We typically had three or four prophetic words and sometimes as many as eight or ten. There were a couple of instances when people were so enthusiastically charged that regretfully the prophesying continued long after God was finished.

Many wonderful things happened in those years, but there were some negative circumstances as well. In the midst of it there were some prophecies that were inaccurate and some true words that were misinterpreted. A true word that is not accurately interpreted or applied can be as dangerous as an inaccurate word of prophecy. For the most part, everyone was left to his own interpretation and application.

People who were around in those days can remember the liberty and excitement of the meetings. All in all, it seemed like a pretty exciting place to be. Someone called our church 'Never a Dull Moment Fellowship'. However, what I remember are the hours and hours of meetings with discouraged people who were disillusioned and hurt. I was receiving a significant education about my naïve approach to leadership where I was letting almost anything be said in the public meetings.

Liberty and structure

There are at least eight basic components that we see as edifying in a normal worship service. There is (1) the worship of God through music, (2) the preaching of the word, (3) testimonies, (4) a ministry time when we pray for the sick and hurting, and the lost, (5) a place for God to speak to the church through the prophetic gifts, (6) fellowship, (7) baptisms and communion, and (8) church business (announcements, tithes, etc.). Some people have the mistaken idea that liberty is simply changing the order of those eight elements. Just because someone decides to change the order of preaching and worship doesn't mean there is a freedom of the Spirit in the church. Liberty, in my understanding, consists of two things. First of all, it is the confidence that people have in their hearts before God. They are assured that they are forgiven and that the Lord is for them, even in their weakness and immaturity. When people sense liberty in their hearts before God without any condemnation, then the church is in a position to grow in the Spirit.

The second part of liberty is the willingness to allow the Holy Spirit to interrupt our schedule. If God wants to send a 'Holy Spirit breeze' across the congregation in an unusual way, then we must allow it. We don't want to be in bondage to our church structure. The church leadership has to be sensitive to the spontaneous wind or direction of the Spirit. If there is no apparent change of direction that God indicates, then be at peace with the normal format. Simply juggling the order of the service does not constitute liberty.

On the other hand, I know some people who consider any kind of structure as a sign of a controlling spirit. In my opinion, God is the author of these eight components of public worship. He likes fellowship, worship, preaching and, yes, even announcements that enhance the necessary communication within a church family. What we do at Metro Vineyard is to 'put up our sail', and if the breeze of the Spirit comes across the church, we try to catch it. We are not, however, under the presumption that an unpredictable 'breeze' needs to break into every gathering. Those eight components are very biblical and represent a healthy overall diet for the church.

We have also noticed that the interruptive breeze of God often comes in seasons. At times we have gone two to three weeks with the service interrupted and redirected by the Holy Spirit every week. Then we will have four to five months in a row in which this almost never happens. There are seasons in the life of a congregation when the Holy Spirit redirects the service according to his specific purposes. He will also 'blow the wind' of his Spirit on the preaching, the worship, the fellowship—on the service in such a way that it does not redirect the order of the service, but simply anoints what is already happening. Some people have the idea that liberty is to reorder the eight components each week. It doesn't take much insight to see through this superficial definition of liberty.

It is naïve to believe that structure and liberty are opposites. I know a number of pastors who do not believe in conforming to a structured meeting. People are permitted to do anything they want, with very few boundaries. That may seem fun for a few months, but by the twelve-month mark it usually becomes tiresome. After everyone has done his thing a dozen times, people aren't usually as excited about so much spontaneity as they once were. God put the gift of leadership into the church for a reason. True, it is not to restrict true liberty, but to facilitate, direct and preserve the flow of life. Much of the flow of life can be enjoyed without changing the order of worship every week.

Procedure at Metro Vineyard Fellowship

Most churches I've visited that allow for the expression of prophetic gifts do so by having a programmed pause for the prophetic. The service begins with exuberant praise, slows down to tender worship songs and finally slows down even more to a silent pause in the service waiting for prophetic words to be given.

There are two types of pause in a worship service. One is a programmed silence to make room for a prophetic word. The other is a time of silence because we sense the presence of God. This is a worshipful silence in which people can commune with God in a private way, unrelated to the programme and direction of the entire church service. The last thing we want at that point is someone shouting out a prophecy. On occasion, we pause for both reasons: to receive a prophetic word and just to enjoy God's presence. We pause out of reverence for God because his presence is there awakening people's hearts.

However, at Metro Vineyard, over the years we have developed a somewhat different method for administrating and making room for the prophetic gifts in a regular worship service. Again the purpose of leadership is to facilitate the flow of life and power. Therefore, we do not always have pauses to wait for prophetic words in our worship service, and spontaneous prophecies are almost never shouted out from the congregation.

We have a microphone at the front row by one of our pastors who has the oversight of prophetic ministry for that meeting. We invite and encourage people to come to the front at any time during the service to speak to the pastor. If the pastor knows the person is credible, he simply hands the microphone to them. If he doesn't know them, he quietly helps them discern if the prophetic word is for the whole church or just for them personally. Also, he seeks to understand if this is the right time to share it. People can have a legitimate prophetic word, but the wrong timing. Maybe it should be shared after the preaching and just before the ministry prayer time instead of during the worship time. If several people approach the pastor at once, he will usually determine in which order the words should be given. Many times several people come with the same word. In this case, the pastor sums them all up and shares it with the church instead of each person giving their words individually. At the proper time, he will attract the attention of the worship leader, who will make a place in the service for the prophetic word. If it seems more appropriate, he may come up and summarise some of the different prophetic words himself, or he may also have one or two of the people come up to the microphone and speak to the whole church.

It is our presumption that in a large congregation which nurtures the prophetic ministry there are going to be 50–100 different people with a dream, vision or prophetic word that they received either in the worship service or throughout the previous week. Just because someone receives a revelation from

God doesn't mean it is to be spoken from the platform. The issue for us is to find a way to discern what God is saying to us and then to communicate it to the congregation in an orderly way. My guess is that a lot of revelation is not intended to be shared publicly, but is, in fact, a personal word for the individual. There may also be ten people who have the same word, dream or vision. Not all ten need to be spoken, but together they are God's way of confirming the facts of the one who gives or summarises the public expression of the prophetic word.

In our current format, there are usually few programmed pauses in our worship services, and there are not very many spontaneous words given from the congregation. The prophetic singers usually express God's prophetic word to us with beautiful songs and music. Normally Michael is the pastor responsible for the leadership of prophetic ministry during the worship services. He is supported by the other members of the leadership team, serving somewhat like an air traffic controller. The gift of leadership in operation here is to facilitate the orderly flow of prophetic revelation.

A couple of hundred people in your congregation who have their spiritual antennae up and who would love to see God interrupt the normal course of every service can be a challenge to your gift of leadership! The worst thing that can happen is for the leaders (who believe it is God's best to stick with the predetermined order) and the people (who desire spontaneous interruptions) to get into a tug of war over this issue. The pastors must be willing to go with the Spirit's flow and, likewise, those sensitive people also need to recognise the legitimate need for the gift of leadership in the God-ordained functioning of the worship service.

When people come to us with some type of prophetic revelation that suggests a significant redirection in the service that is not apparent to all, we will usually tell them that we are going to wait for some other confirmation. Second Corinthians 13:1

says, 'By the mouth of two or three witnesses every word shall be established.' I understand that neither this verse nor its Old Testament source (Deut 19:15) is primarily focused on judging prophetic words. Nevertheless, we follow a principle of confirming major course corrections in our worship service by two or three witnesses. This confirming principle is alluded to in 1 Corinthians 14:29: 'Let two or three prophets speak, and let the others judge.' Usually there are prophetic confirmations when God wants to change the direction of the service.

Correcting unanointed prophecies

Most pastors and leaders have at one time or another experienced the fear of strange or unbiblical words being voiced in the church in the name of prophecy. But if there is an established process of correcting such fleshly words, there will be less pressure on both the leaders and the people.

There are several different types of correction that will periodically need to be employed. Although most of the prophetic words in our church come through the microphone up front, that procedure is not established as a hard and fast rule. Asking people to speak their prophetic word over the microphone serves three purposes. First, it allows the entire congregation to hear the word clearly. Secondly, it gives us the ability to tape record it. Thirdly, it gives the leaders a chance to talk with the person when necessary before the prophetic word is spoken. However, someone will occasionally give a word from the congregation that does not edify the body; there seems to be no inspiration, no life or relevance. I do not like to call this a false prophecy, for that might imply that the person is deceived by a demon. In 1 Corinthians 14:3 it says,'He who prophesies speaks edification and exhortation and comfort.' The word may not do any of those things, but if it's not a directional prophecy, and if it doesn't represent a doctrinal error, then even though it is unanointed we treat it as a less serious problem.

We will usually let it go the first time and probably the second. However, after two so-called prophetic words that seem to contain no anointing or edification, we will go to the person and gently suggest that they submit their word to the leaders sitting at the front. If it happens a third time, we then *require* them to submit their prophetic words to the leadership before speaking then out in the church service. If the person does not heed this third private correction from the leadership, we will stop them on the fourth time and correct them publicly. This has only happened a few times in twelve years. On each occasion we have taken time to explain to the entire congregation the process that evolved with that person. If the whole process is not explained to the congregation, then other prophetic people may have a paralysing fear of being publicly corrected. But when the people understand the whole process, it gives them security to know that the leadership will not deal harshly with them if they make a mistake when they begin to step out. They must not be afraid that they might prophesy something wrong and be suddenly corrected for it before the whole church. The church needs to be able to trust the leadership to deal with such things in a spirit of gentleness or else the spirit of faith and liberty in the church will diminish quickly. If this happens, then the prophetic ministry will surely dry up and shut down.

Instant correction

There are two types of prophetic word that we publicly correct *immediately*, but as gently as possible. The first type is a prophetic utterance given as a rebuke or correction to the church without first going through our leadership team. For example, I would never go to another church and give a prophetic word that was a correction or redirection without giving it first to their leadership. If the leadership of the church agree with the word, I would ask them to present it to the church. It is usually more effective if the local leadership team speak the corrective word instead of a visitor, who is not well known by the local church. However, they might ask me to share it with the church, but I would do so only after it was made clear to everyone that I was speaking at their request. If, in our private discussion, the leaders rejected the prophetic word, yet I was convinced that I had unmistakably heard from God, I might warn them in the pastor's office, 'I think you people are in real trouble.' But I would never speak a corrective word publicly in a church outside their leadership and authority structure.

If a person stands up and gives a prophetic word that suggests a new direction, a rebuke or correction for our church without first submitting it to the leadership, I would desire to respond gently in this way: 'I appreciate the fact that you are trying to hear from God for this church and that you care about us. However, I would like you to take this word, share it with the leadership team and let us discern it together. We also invite you to be a part of this process if you wish, but for now we are not going to move in that direction. We will come back and give you a report later.' It is very important to teach people to stay within proper lines of spiritual authority when bringing a corrective or directive word to a local church.

The other type of prophetic word we would correct immediately is one that contains unorthodox doctrinal implications. Again the correction must be done with kindness and gentleness. This is not the time for the pastor to seek to look macho by showing how many bullets he has in his pastoral gun. We must always remember that we are dealing with precious human beings who are redeemed by Jesus' precious blood. If you deal harshly with the individual's error, that harshness will also destroy the liberty and openness in the church. If a person's prophecy included some kind of significant doctrinal error, then I would have to correct it on the spot. I would begin by saying, 'I'm sure he meant well, but the word spoken calls into question a doctrine that we esteem as biblical.' Then I would clearly state the accurate doctrine that was called into question.

God speaks through us

It is such a simple idea: God wants to speak to and through the body of Christ. The power of revelation can even flow through the youngest believer in the church. The church is made up of people who are all indwelt with the power and presence of the Holy Spirit. No one has a corner on the Holy Spirit who sovereignly moves in and through the church as he desires. Our procedures are not perfect, but on occasion they work well to facilitate the power and revelation of the Spirit operating through the church as a whole.

Recently, a dear lady in our congregation came up to Michael Sullivant. It seemed obvious to him that she was being moved on by the Holy Spirit. She was very urgent and emotionally charged, which is not her natural inclination. She said that the Lord was showing her that there were some people present that morning who needed to come to Jesus for salvation, and that the Lord was going to move upon them. She offered to share this word publicly, but Michael didn't discern that this would be the best thing. Rather, he briefly shared with me the prophetic word and left it in my hands to administrate. At the end of my sermon, because of this prophetic word, I gave a salvation invitation and five people immediately responded. I then shared with the congregation that this prophetic word had been given to one of our members earlier that morning. This just added to the joy of the whole event in the hearts of our people.

Although this kind of thing has happened from time to time

at Metro Vineyard Fellowship, it is not a weekly occurrence. However, on another occasion, after the preaching, during a ministry time, Michael was in the front of the church as usual, collecting words of knowledge from the people to speak over the microphone. People were coming forward in a response to receive personal prayer. At one point I prayed for a certain lady. As I began to pray, nothing seemed to be happening. This went on for five minutes or so. At this point, Michael shared a word of knowledge over the microphone given by one of our members about a dysfunctional pancreas. The lady I was praying for said to me that this prophetic word was for her. Up to this point, I was simply praying for the Lord to touch her in a general way. Then suddenly she began to feel God's power move upon her body and she became unsure of what to do. I later found out that she was a first-time visitor who had been brought to the service by a friend and that she had never seen anything like this before. That was why she was anxious. I encouraged her to calm down and explained to her that it was the power of the Holy Spirit that was touching her and she didn't need to be afraid. As I spoke to her, she opened her eyes and started screaming and crying. She seemed to be looking behind me and started crying out, 'I can see! I can see!' I had no idea what was going on. As it turned out, she had had a large blind spot over one of her eyes due to diabetes, and it had instantly gone away as we prayed that morning. The Lord had used that prophetic word of knowledge from one of the people in the congregation to spark a marvellous healing. The church rejoiced greatly in praise to the Lord that day.

These are just a couple of illustrations of how God is using what may generally be termed 'the prophetic' in our midst and how we have been led to administrate it in our services.

12

The Prophetic Song of the Lord

The nature and power of music

Music is a heavenly thing in its essence; a part of creation that reflects and proceeds from the very heart and personality of God himself. This makes music prophetic in nature. Our Father loves music. He is a singing God (Zeph 3:17). And he has a powerful voice. Jesus, the Son, composed the song of all songs that will be eternally fresh—the 'Song of the Lamb' (Rev 15:3–4). The Holy Spirit inspires songs and melodies. There is a whole book of them in the Bible; the book of Psalms, along with the greatest song in redemptive history, the Song of Solomon. The Scriptures reveal that music existed within the angelic realm before the creation of the earth (Job 38:7). It has always provided a means of communion and connection between God and his creatures above and below. Spirit-filled Christians are to occupy themselves with singing psalms, hymns and spiritual songs, singing and making melodies in their hearts to the Lord (Eph 5:18).

Music has intrinsic power to move the inner affections and the outer actions of people. It is a providential gift that God has given to all peoples and even to some of the animals. It is pleasant to hear the birds sing on a beautiful spring day. It is true that music is a source of power that Satan has always sought to usurp, pervert and use for his assault against God and his kingdom, but this is actually a testimony to its great value. Satan has used the spiritual force and influence of music to seduce and lead people into idolatry, vanity and sexual immorality through the ages, and has done so quite effectively. Yet God is not intimidated by this fact and he refuses to allow the thief to possess it as his own. God still owns all the real and true life-giving music of both heaven and earth.

What is the prophetic song of the Lord?

In light of these things, it should not surprise us that God has used minstrels to inspire and activate the prophetic (2 Kings 3:15). Neither should it be surprising that prophetically inspired people will be led to sing in the Spirit, communicating the heart of God to his people and the heart of his people back to God. Through the years God has blessed our fellowship with a number of men and women who have composed, played and sung many inspired songs. Many prophetic songs were received by these people in the context of our regular intercessory prayer meetings. In Hebrews 2:12, the Scripture implies that one of the deepest longings within the heart of Jesus is to sing the praises of his Father in the midst of and through the instrumentality of the congregation of the believing: 'I will declare Your name to My brethren; in the midst of the assembly I will sing praise to You' (Heb 2:12).

This is the essence of the 'song of the Lord'. The risen Christ loves to impart some of the passion he has for his Father to the hearts of his younger brothers and sisters as he imparts his songs to them by the Spirit to glorify his Father. The Westminster Catechism begins with the famous statement, 'The chief end of man is to glorify God and enjoy Him for ever.' (So much for Puritans being down on pleasure!) American pastor and author, John Piper, has brilliantly changed this sentence to say, 'The chief end of man is to glorify God by enjoying Him for ever.' I can't think of any better way of enjoying God, than by experiencing the pleasure of mingling the very love that Jesus has for the Father with Spirit-inspired music. Surely some of the 'pleasures that are at His right hand for evermore' will be the heavenly music and songs that surround his throne.

Many people who have had heavenly encounters, and have returned to tell about it, have spoken about the marvellous music they heard in heaven. Also, many people who have had experiences of having their ears open to the Spirit realm have testified to hearing the angelic choirs and music. In fact, I had an experience like this myself. Early one morning a few years ago, I arrived at the church auditorium to attend an intercessory prayer meeting. As I got out of my car and approached the building, I heard this tremendous music coming from the sanctuary. I thought that the people who had gathered were listening to some wonderful music tape like Handel's *Messiah* on the sound system at a very high volume. The sound was loud and majestic. I continued to hear this awesome music up until the moment I opened the sanctuary door. The glorious music was instantly shut off, just as if someone had pushed the stop button on the stereo. To my surprise, the sound system was not yet on, and the few people who had arrived early for the meeting were quietly waiting for the worship team to arrive. They had heard nothing. I was stunned to realise that I had just had an encounter with the Holy Spirit. I didn't tell anyone at the meeting what I had heard. In anticipation, I thought, surely the Lord is going to visit and especially bless this meeting in power. That must be why he let me hear the heavenly music, but to my surprise, it was just like most of the ordinary prayer meetings that we conduct each day—nothing spectacular, just some tired but sincere believers calling out to their God at an early morning hour.

Afterwards, as I pondered the meaning of my experience that morning, I realised what God was saying. He was blessed by those 'ordinary' daily prayer meetings that to us, most often, seemed weak and unanointed. The heavenly hosts, under the Holy Spirit's direction, are apparently regularly gathering at prayer meetings, unseen and unperceived, to mingle our weak prayers and praises with their strong and glorious heavenly music, worship and prayer. I figure that the angelic choir may really help our voices sound more beautiful in the rarefied air of heaven. I am actually grateful that the prayer meeting that morning was ordinary. It built my faith and gave more significance to all the time I've spent in 'dry' intercession. This story has also encouraged other believers to persevere in prayer. Maybe the Lord always adds the voices of his angelic choir as our day's intercession reaches his throne. We are not responsible for making our prayers anointed; we're just supposed to pray and not give up!

Jesus promises to proclaim the Father's name as he sings in the midst of the congregation (Heb 2:12). This implies the Holy Spirit giving the church a deeper revelation of the nature and personality of God in prophetic messages through song. It also implies extolling and declaring the majesty and beauty of God and his ways through prophetic prayers that are sung. In Romans 8:26, it states that the Holy Spirit who resides within believers helps them communicate the depths of their being to God in prayer that is in harmony with his will. In 1 Corinthians 2:10–11, Paul says that the Holy Spirit also searches out the very depths of God and reveals his thoughts to believers. The Holy Spirit is the communication link between God and his people. Perhaps an aspect of the depths of God is a treasury of heavenly music that the Holy Spirit will impart to prophetic musicians within the body of Christ for the blessing of all mankind and the furthering of God's kingdom. This music will reflect a full range of the attributes of our awesome God, from his tender mercy to his terrible judgements. This is really nothing new, in that he has been releasing his songs throughout the centuries. Some of these songs are spontaneous as they are sung for the first and only time in worship services, prayer meetings, home groups or private devotional times. On the other hand, many prophetic songs have been written down and even recorded to be heard over and over as worship songs or hymns used by choirs, Sunday worship services or as solos. Still, I think there will be an intensification of the Spirit's work in releasing his songs before the Second Coming of Jesus.

The book of Revelation indicates that God's work and Satan's work both take on new levels of manifestation and power just before the end of the age. I view it as a cosmic and earthly clash of holy and unholy passions. Attending the increase of prophetic ministry will undoubtedly be an increase of inspired prophetic music to impart passion for Jesus and his Father in the hearts of believers. Undoubtedly, the enemy will give an increasing counterfeit anointing to musicians and songs that will draw people's allegiances after him and his unholy spirits.

The Scripture exhorts us to sing a new song unto the Lord. The Holy Spirit stands ready to anoint and inspire many prophetic musicians and singers who will risk getting so intimate with the Godhead that they will discern the fresh music of heaven and release it to us for our enjoyment, refreshment, instruction and admonition.

Twelve practical helps

Following are some of the things we have learned through the years that help define the banks of this musical river of prophetic music that flows through the church. It is important that spiritual leaders help define some tracks for believers to run on when it comes to this subjective experience of prophetic singing.

1. Sing to the Lord in your private devotions. Sing the Scriptures. Sing in the Spirit. Sing what is in your heart. Sing your prayers. You will in this way discover if the Lord is periodically anointing you with prophetic songs, and thus your confidence will grow so that you may sing them out in public worship settings. For those of us who are never called to sing publicly, it will be spiritually edifying to us and pleasurable to the Lord, even if it could only be called at best a 'joyful noise'!

2. I believe that God is pleased for us to do some 'holy risk-taking' in safe settings, where we will sing these spontaneous songs out loud before other people. One way to become accustomed to this type of spontaneous singing is in small group settings like the worship time during a home fellowship group or a prayer meeting. Your friends can give you loving feedback on the impact, good or bad, that you are making in your spontaneous singing. Heed their advice and encouragement. We have found our intercessory prayer meetings and home groups a wonderful place to test the waters.

3. If you begin to sing out publicly, it is wise to start by singing songs to God rather than songs from God. You will avoid the extra pressure that necessarily comes with the claim of directly speaking on God's behalf. I encourage the prophetic singers to seek to sense the particular heart cry the Holy Spirit is anointing as the congregation worships with a heightened sense of inspiration on various songs, then to sing a prayer back to God that captures that particular mode as discerned through the songs God anoints in that service. It may be a cry for mercy, a lament of failure, an expression of gratitude, an expression of joyful celebration, a search for truth, or a song that recites any number of spiritual postures and moods that occur in the lives of God's people. You can often discern when the congregation feels that added inspiration as the worship leader touches these themes in his selection of worship songs. It is very easy to sing

a spontaneous song back to God that reflects the songs and themes the Holy Spirit has already anointed in that worship service.

4. Use the Bible as a glossary for the kinds of words and phrases that you can draw upon in singing prophetically. The Psalms are an obvious place in which to meditate to store up this kind of inspirational material. I may also encourage our prophetic singers to sing straight out of the Psalms. If prophetic singers will immerse themselves in meditation on Scripture, then their prophesying in song will become richer, fuller and more anointed. God has already anointed his written word.

5. Don't feel that to sing prophetically you must only sing spontaneous songs. God can give prophetic songs ahead of time just as well as on the spot. You may even simply sing a Scripture passage that God seems to be highlighting in that moment or season. Old and well-known songs alike can often have a prophetic edge placed on them under the creative leadership of the Holy Spirit. Many times a musical instrument can even be used prophetically. For years we have had an undeniably anointed saxophone player in our midst, who has blessed us repeatedly by spontaneously playing during worship services.

6. Be prepared for mistakes to occur from time to time. Usually they won't be so bad that attention needs to be drawn to them. Administrating this ministry is virtually the same as dealing with prophetic utterances in general. If leaders establish a spiritual atmosphere so tight that mistakes can never be made or tolerated, then they probably won't have anyone in their midst with the fortitude to grow in prophetic singing or in spontaneous instrumental solos.

7. Church leaders need to teach publicly on prophetic singing from time to time in order to place value upon it and stir the faith and courage of the prophetic singers and musicians. If leaders will sow, then they will also reap. All things are subject

to the law of entropy and we need to put energy into the things that we believe in so that their expression doesn't fizzle out. It can also be helpful to host a weekend seminar for your worship team where you bring in outside worship leaders who are experienced in prophetic music. Have these visiting prophetic worship leaders teach and model prophetic music. Then have them lay their hands on those who desire to be released in prophetic music. This can be imparted from one believer to another by the Holy Spirit (1 Tim 4:14). We can assist churches in this by sending a prophetic worship leader or musician to them for a weekend. Your church will be significantly blessed once the music is blessed with a prophetic anointing on it.

8. Worship leaders need to make room for prophetic songs during worship services. If they simply pause a few times during the singing part of a worship service, while continuing to play a discernible chord progression, the prophetic singers will know when to sing out and will be able to sing in harmony with the instruments. As time goes by, the worship team will learn to work together in an undistracted manner.

9. We have found, as a rule, that a maximum of three to four prophetic songs is enough for most worship services. There can be exceptions. We have celebration services once a month on Sunday nights where we worship for two to three hours, along with inviting the Holy Spirit's ministry to heal and refresh people. At these more intensive worship settings, we may have more than three or four songs because the worship lasts several hours. The singers in a regular Sunday morning service should limit themselves to one to two minutes and one to two general themes. There are exceptions to this, but if these guidelines are generally followed then prophetic singing won't be 'overdone'. If it becomes too common and over-used then it can become an object of scorn.

10. Prophetic songs should be limited to the boundaries of exhortation, encouragement and comfort as described in

1 Corinthians 14:3. They shouldn't become a vehicle for bringing correction or direction to the body unless the governing leaders of the church have agreed to it in advance.

11. We encourage prophetic singers to seek to bring forth clear and simple messages. Prophecy in the church needs to trumpet a distinct sound. They should definitely seek to avoid messages that are too mystical, parabolic or complicated. We have had to ask a few of our singers to avoid using language that is heavily symbolic and to express themselves in simple themes that are easily understood by all.

12. Encourage the people who have a singing or instrumental gift to test the waters in this kind of ministry. God may have given them their singing voice and musical ability for a prophetic purpose. Discourage those who don't have the voice for it to refrain from singing their prophecies in public settings. They, like myself, need to stick to talking!

13

Revelation, Interpretation and Application

Practically everyone filled with God's Spirit is able to prophesy on an inspirational level, especially in a worship service where the Holy Spirit's presence is more easily recognised. The result of what we call *inspirational prophecy* is described by Paul this way: 'He who prophesies speaks edification and exhortation and comfort to men' (1 Cor 14:3). The purpose of this type of prophecy is to inspire and refresh our hearts without giving any correction or new direction. This kind of prophecy is usually a reminder from the heart of God about his care and purpose for us, to emphasise some truth we already know from the Bible. Inspirational prophecy can be a very profound revelation, or it can be (as it usually is) something very simple––'I feel the Lord is saying that he really loves us.' That message, if it is given at a divinely prescribed time, can be powerful and effective.

Since this is a type of revelation that can flow through every believer, leaders have to use restraint. There are times in worship services when the Holy Spirit moves in a way that everyone can sense. If the pastor doesn't exercise some leadership, forty people will line up to give an inspirational word. If inspirational prophecy occurs too frequently, it will become too common and people will no longer pay attention to what is being said. They will, in a sense, begin to 'despise prophesying', and not without good reason. When you have an overload of inspirational prophecy, the worst thing is that the congregation will often miss the simple but timely word that is designed to give people a fresh inspiration from the heart of God.

Small groups provide the opportunity for people to experience and participate in this kind of prophecy that focuses on inspiration rather than correction or new direction. In our larger worship gatherings, we generally pray that God will impart prophetic words through the worship leaders. They can also share what they are hearing with some of the leaders sitting at the front. We have come to the conclusion that it is best to limit and restrain inspirational prophecy so that its overuse does not undermine its effectiveness.

Other kinds of prophecy that go beyond inspiration to include correction or direction need to be administrated even more carefully. Our church has received many significant benefits as a result of directional prophecy. However, the ability of any church to receive these benefits hinges on a willingness to wade through the process of discerning not only the initial revelation but the proper interpretation and finally the correct application. Prophetic ministry can dynamically affect the spiritual temperature of your church, but if you don't concentrate on the interpretation and application of the prophecy, you may be headed for trouble.

Interpreting divine information

We use the term 'revelation' to refer to the essence of the information that is communicated—no more, no less. It is the raw data of divine communication. The problems we have had to deal with have not been the result of incorrect prophetic revelation. In most cases, the information was right, but the problems began when someone went on to incorrectly assume what the prophetic revelation meant.

This misinterpretation can begin either with the person receiving the prophetic revelation or with the person to whom it is directed. Let me give an example. In a public meeting, a prophetic minister spoke the following prophetic word to a man whom he had never met: 'You have a music ministry. You're called to be a singer. . .' The prophetic minister actually saw musical notes around the person in a vision. Obviously the prophetic minister thought the man was called by God to sing or to play an instrument, but the person to whom the revelation was directed didn't play or sing at all. He was the owner of a music shop. When we took the prophetic minister aside and questioned him, his response was, 'Well, how was I supposed to know?'

That is *precisely* the point. He wasn't supposed to know. It seemed obvious to him that the person would be in the music ministry as a performer. However, when you start making an assumption on prophetic revelation based on what seems obvious, you might get into trouble.

It is easy to cross over the line of receiving the revelation to the interpretation of that revelation without even realising it. As a pastor and as a team leader, you must constantly remind yourself to distinguish between the raw data (divine information) and the interpretation of its content. Many people are disillusioned over the fact that they may not have seen the prophetic revelation come to pass. In many cases, the prophecy simply did not come to pass as they assumed or interpreted that it would. The problem was that they allowed the two (revelation and interpretation) to run together in their mind until they could no longer distinguish between what God had actually said and the expectation created by their interpretation.

The interpretation of revelation is often contrary to the obvious. The scribes and Pharisees were perfect examples of this. The tradition of the elders was more than a collection of their customs. It was the theological interpretation of the *Torah*, the first five books of the Old Testament. Years later those traditions were written down in what is called the *Talmud*. To the scribes and Pharisees, Jesus was a law-breaker because he did not keep the traditions of the elders. These religious leaders could no longer distinguish between revelation (the *Torah*) and interpretation (the *Talmud*). To them, the interpretations and applications were obvious and indisputable. This is a tendency that shows up in every generation. Many people who are 'into' end-time prophecy have become so wrapped up in their charts and predictions that they can no longer distinguish between the raw data of biblical revelation and their systematic interpretations. The Pharisees also misinterpreted the prophets' revelation and missed the purpose of God because Jesus came in a way contrary to all their expectations.

One of the characteristics of prophetic revelation is that it is sometimes allegorical or symbolic, and is fully understood only after future events have taken place. From the Old Testament perspective, it was not altogether clear what the Messiah would look like. The prophets foretold the coming of both a kingly Messiah and a suffering Servant, but no one even remotely considered that both were the same person. Obviously kingly messiahs aren't servants, and they don't suffer. Even the disciples had a hard time with it. The Synoptic Gospels (Matthew, Mark and Luke) are written in a present tense setting. In other words, they show how baffled the disciples were. The Messianic Secret is a theme that runs throughout all the Synoptic Gospels. They had a very difficult time figuring out who he was and the nature of his eternal kingdom.

The Gospel of John was possibly written around AD 90 and looks back at Jesus from a post-resurrection perspective. In John's Gospel, there is no mystery about Jesus' identity. Clear affirmations of his deity are found in the first verse and throughout the entire book.

For the disciples, and even for some of the Pharisees and scribes, the interpretation of prophetic revelation that was obscure when it was happening became crystal clear after the foretold events had taken place. We have to be careful about locking in on our interpretation of prophetic revelation lest we miss what God is trying to say to us and do with us.

If you carelessly interpret prophetic revelation, you might cause chaos in someone's life. Over time we have gained insight concerning the administration of prophetic ministry. We have, however, in that learning process naïvely allowed some unfortunate things to happen. We had a situation that turned into a pastoral nightmare. It was the result of a wrong interpretation being applied to an authentic prophetic revelation. One of our prophetic people received a word from the Lord for a man in our congregation. This man was horrified when the prophetic minister publicly shared that he had no integrity in his finances.

I happened to be out of town that morning. That's not to say it wouldn't have happened if I was there. The problem was that we were naïve about the process of dealing with corrective prophecies.

When I returned, I went to the prophetic minister and asked him exactly what he had seen. He told me that he had seen a dark cloud over the area of the man's finances. He had interpreted this to mean that the man was stealing money, but this interpretation was totally wrong! What actually happened was that soon afterwards the man's business partner embezzled a large sum of money from him. The prophetic word was a warning to the man to watch out for someone who might steal money from him, but it was mistakenly pronounced as a judgement against him. The brother was humiliated publicly by the prophetic word and a resulting shadow was cast over his integrity.

First of all, the prophetic revelation should never have been given publicly. If the man was guilty of financial sin, then he should have been approached privately, as called for in Matthew 18. If we had interpreted the prophetic word accurately as a warning to help the man, instead of a judgement against him, it would have been spoken differently. If we had properly distinguished between the revelation and the interpretation, perhaps the warning could have prevented the financial loss.

Revelation and confirmation

When you receive a prophetic word from someone, you must hold it at arm's length until God himself confirms it in your heart. If a prophetic minister receives accurate and authentic revelation from God that a person is going to have a street ministry, all they are doing is giving the person concerned advance warning that he or she will personally hear a new direction from God about a street ministry. This prophetic notification is sometimes God's way of confirming ahead of time what you will hear for yourself later on. On other occasions, prophetic words confirm something you have already heard very clearly, but you cannot step out and act on the prophetic word alone if you haven't received the confirmation. Often when people act on a new direction before receiving the confirmation, they get off track. Many times the accurate and often unexpected interpretation is clarified in the process of the confirmation.

One of the reasons we require all directional prophecy to go through the leadership is that it would be awkward to go through the process of properly interpreting the word in the middle of a public worship service. I often hear prophetic words in churches or conferences I attend as a visitor. I would have all kinds of questions about some of the words that go unchallenged. You can't interrogate people every time they say something prophetic, but you had better question them carefully if the prophetic word involves a new direction for you! It is important that you know and keep in mind what is put forth as divine revelation, what is confirmed and what is assumed to be the interpretation. If you don't distinguish between these three elements, and keep those lines clear in your mind, you will undoubtedly trip over your own misconceptions.

When a person receives a prophetic revelation that speaks about their future promotion in natural or spiritual things, they must guard their hearts. It is easy to have wrong assumptions, and then to run with things we have no business running with. Sometimes, it is our selfish ambition that causes us to set our hearts on things that the Lord did not confirm. Prophetic words that promise us future promotion can fall on us like petrol on a fire. We so long for those words to be accurate. The basic problems are not always with the prophetic words or with the people who give them. It is sometimes our selfish ambition that gets us into trouble. If our eyes are completely on the Lord, then we're not as prone to falling for words that promise us great honour. Sometimes I've been more interested in running with the word than really knowing if it was truly from God.

A man with an ambitious heart is always vulnerable when it comes to an exaggerated or flattering prophetic word. Problems associated with prophetic ministry are sometimes rooted in ambition, either in the prophetic minister who exaggerates or the ambitious recipient who refuses to wait for the confirmation or the proper interpretation.

If a prophetic minister adds his own commentary and interpretation to the basic revelation he has received from God, then someone is eventually going to end up confused and disappointed. The same is true if a person accepts the word of the prophet without a confirmation. Proverbs 13:12 says, 'Hope deferred makes the heart sick.' It also makes the person angry.

There are Christians who are unaware of the fact that they are angry with God. They may have become cynical, critical, angry people who bite and devour others in the body of Christ. The problem could be that they are heartsick over unfulfilled hopes and expectations, and in a heart that is sick with disappointment, all kinds of heartache can develop. If we are not careful to interpret prophetic revelation, we can end up with many heartsick people.

People who feel disillusioned and offended by God will eventually lose their spiritual vigour. It doesn't often happen over night, but it does eventually happen. To drive a wedge between you and God is precisely what the enemy wants to do. He tried to cause Job to be offended at God by tempting Job to interpret his circumstances incorrectly.

The application of prophetic revelation

The last step in our process of prophetic administration is application. The interpretation answers the question: What does the revelation mean? The application answers the question: When and how will this come to pass? as well as: What should I do?

The anointing and grace to receive revelation is not the same as the anointing and grace to discern the interpretation. We have people who interpret prophetic revelation with much greater clarity than the people who receive the revelation. Another distinct grace from God is the ability to apply what has been interpreted. We have a council of prophetic people that is regularly involved with this.

I have not met very many prophetic people who have much wisdom on the application end of the process. I have seen some of the more seasoned prophetic ministers receive words from the Lord that predicted the timing of events with great precision. Nevertheless, the person with the revelation rarely knows the timing. Bob Jones has an incredible gift of revelation, but he would tell you himself that he often tends to miss it on interpretation and application. One time Bob gave a person a word along with the phrase, 'By the end of the year.' Well, the end of the year came and the prophecy had not come to pass. I went back to Bob and questioned him about it. It turns out that 'by the end of the year' was not a part of the revelation. 'Well,' said Bob, 'why would the Lord give it if it wasn't going to happen by the end of the year?' My reply was, 'I can think of a dozen reasons!'

Revelation itself is not going to help the body unless it goes through the process of interpretation and application. Again, the application is the action that should be taken based on the interpretation. The interpretation may be accurate, but if a person jumps the gun and gets ahead of God in the application, a considerable amount of hurt and confusion may result. Consequently, there is as much need for divine wisdom in the interpretation and application as there is in the revelation. God never works as fast as people think he should. Don't get involved with prophetic people and words if you are not willing to wait on God to bring them to pass. God will declare his intention through the prophetic gift, but if the application is not in his timing, you'll find yourself trying to step through a door that is not open. The way is not yet prepared and the grace is not yet sufficient.

Another aspect of the application is: Who should be told the revelation and interpretation and when should they be told? The following questions must be answered: 'Is it something for the entire congregation, or only the leadership, or is it something that shouldn't be spoken at all?' Joseph learned the hard way that telling his brothers about his prophetic dreams could get him into trouble. His brothers interpreted the dreams accurately and came up with their own application—they got rid of Joseph! Like Joseph, many people have a hard time keeping to themselves what they have heard from God. It's our nature to want others to know that *God* has a special plan for us.

The same thing is true of the person through whom prophetic revelation comes. The prophetic person often feels he should tell everyone immediately. He wants everyone to know he was the one who received special revelation so he will receive the credit for it. That sounds pretty ambitious, but it is often a motive in the person's heart of which he is unaware.

Prophetic people who strive to receive recognition usually wind up being corrected. I understand the reasons why they have that tendency, but it's still selfish ambition. The indisputable sign that a person has a wrong motivation is that he or she is pushy. A striving, pushy person with revelation is an unbroken vessel. They don't care about counsel or unity or the wisdom of others. I've learned to stay clear of that kind of prophetic person. If you let them have the microphone three or four times, they will end up bringing unnecessary division to the body.

The most important thing is to get the word to the right people in the proper manner. The way we present things to the congregation often leaves them not even knowing who originally received the word from the Lord. The prophetic person may feel let down and will try to find a way of letting people know that he was the one who received the word. His discernment and perspective on how to apply prophetic revelation is influenced by his need for people to know that he is hearing from God in a special way. Unfortunately, people usually know what is really going on and will disdain the selfish ambition they see in the prophetic person. One of the reasons these people need to be involved in a church that both nurtures and administrates the prophetic is that they often fall into this negative pattern without realising it.

I've had my share of controversy over prophets and prophetic ministry. There are times when people sincerely think they are hearing from God, but are completely mistaken. Nevertheless, the problems in the church caused by prophetic ministry are *almost always* caused, not by incorrect prophecies, but by presumptuous interpretations and applications. Churches need to take the time to learn to work through the process of administrating prophetic ministry and prophetic revelation, for the benefits to the local church are too great and the consequences of shutting it out are too severe.

14

Women as Prophetic Ministers

The ministry of women in the church is a hotly debated topic in many circles today. Unfortunately, the effectiveness of the church has been greatly diminished because the ministry of women has been so limited. The intransigent and sometimes chauvinistic position of some in the church is a result of long-held stereotypes about women, dysfunctional male–female relationships and a truncated view of early church history. My purpose here is neither to put forth a comprehensive theological framework for women in ministry, nor to attempt an exegesis of the New Testament texts that relate to the role of women in the church. There are several excellent books written on this subject. My purpose here is to cite some examples of what has happened in Scripture and church history, and how women function today in prophetic ministry at Metro Vineyard Fellowship in Kansas City.

Whatever your position on the place of women in a teaching or preaching ministry, it is clear that the Scriptures teach that women can and should prophesy.

Women throughout church history

The significant involvement of women in the ministry of Jesus

205

is well documented. They were the witnesses of his crucifixion and resurrection when males were conspicuously absent. Luke declares that the women who had followed Jesus from Galilee still followed along as Christ was carried to the tomb. Matthew tells how they kept watch over the sepulchre after the men had left. John records that the group of people immediately beneath the cross consisted of three women and one man. Though it broke all kinds of social and religious traditions, Jesus made a point to include women in his ministry.

There is little wonder that the prominence of women continued in the development of the early church. A number of women served as leaders in the house churches that were part of the larger church in the city of Rome. Some of those mentioned are Priscilla, Chloe, Lydia, Apphia, Nympha, the mother of John Mark and possibly the 'elect lady' of John's second epistle. Paul mentions Phoebe and refers to her as 'a servant [literally deaconess] of the church in Cenchrea' (Rom 16:1). Paul also mentions Junia, and refers to her as being 'of note among the apostles' (Rom 16:7). Some have debated the exact meaning of this verse. Until the Middle Ages, the identity of Junia as a female apostle was unquestioned. Later translators attempted to change the gender by changing the name to Junias.[1]

There were also women who functioned as prophetic ministers. Philip, selected to serve the apostles as one of the seven and the head of the church in Caesarea, had four virgin daughters who were recognised as prophetesses in the church (Acts 21:8–9). Some believe that these prophetesses became the standard and model for prophetic ministers in the early church. When Pope Militiades proclaimed that two female followers of Montanus were heretics, he contrasted them with Philip's daughters. Militiades explained that their problem was not that

---

[1] *Christian History* (Vol. VII, no. 1, issue 17), p. 7.

they were women prophets, but rather that they were false prophets. Eusebius mentions one Quadratus, a man famous in the second century, who 'shared with the daughters of Philip the distinction of a prophetic gift' (III. 37).[1]

The church quickly spread from its birth place in Jerusalem into areas where the predominant culture was pagan, Greco–Roman or both. In this setting, women commonly held high positions and influence in social, political and religious circles. Women having a leading influence in the church was therefore not thought of in negative terms. About AD 112, the Roman governor, Pliny the Younger, wrote about his efforts to deal with the Christians in Bithynia. He found it necessary to interrogate the leaders of the church, two slave women called *ministrae*, or deaconesses.[2]

There are countless examples of women who served the church with complete and tireless devotion or who, without flinching, endured terrible tortures and martyrdom. A significant step in the process of Christianity gaining political and social dominance in Rome was the large number of female converts among the upper class. Men were less likely to become Christians because doing so would cause them to lose their status in society. An inordinate number of upper-class women is perhaps the reason that Callistus, Bishop of Rome in AD 220, attempted to give women of the senatorial class an ecclesiastical sanction to marry slaves of freedmen.

These high-born women seized the opportunity to become students of the word. One of these was a fourth-century woman named Marcella. The great scholar, Jerome, who translated the Bible into Latin (known as the Vulgate), did not hesitate to refer church leaders to Marcella for help in solving their

---

[1] *Christian History* (vol. VII, no. 1, issue 17), p. 14.
[2] *Ibid*, p.8.

hermeneutical problems.[1]

Women enjoyed great freedom of expression in the earliest days of the church. As time went on, various problems they faced were dealt with in such a way that the original freedom and liberty in the church were replaced by a more precisely defined code of conduct. With each new and more detailed explanation of what was and was not acceptable, the role of women was restricted and diminished.[2]

Nevertheless, even through the Middle Ages there were women who were outstanding examples of spirituality and dedication. The Waldensians, a group beginning in the twelfth century that could be described as Protestants 400 years before the Reformation, were charged with, among other things, allowing women to preach. Catherine of Siena (1347–1380) was a resolute servant to the poor, a Doctor of the Church and a lover of God, whose theology and piety were revered even by the reformers.

One summer when Joan of Arc was about thirteen, she suddenly saw a bright light and heard voices while working in the fields. The voices, which Joan thought were either angels or saints, continued after that day, instructing her to help the Dauphin (France's rightful king) and to save France. With six knights she rode over 300 miles across enemy territory to tell Charles the Dauphin of her plans. When Joan entered the large hall, the Dauphin had disguised himself as one of those in the crowd. Joan walked right up to him and addressed him.

'I am not the Dauphin,' Charles replied.

Joan responded, 'In God's name, gentle sire, you are.' Then she proceeded to reveal to him his private thoughts. The nineteen-year-old girl led the French forces, saved France, and Charles was restored to the throne. Mark Twain studied the life

---

[1] *Christian History* (Vol. VII, no. 1, issue 17), p. 6.
[2] Ibid, pp. 20–24.

of Joan of Arc for twelve years and concluded that her life was 'the most noble life that was ever born into this world save only One'.

Though it is impossible to discern clearly between legend, facts and spiritual anointing, Joan's prophetic experiences seem somewhat similar to those of others I know who have been called to the prophetic ministry.

Women have also played a significant role in the spread and development of Protestantism, particularly in the area of foreign missions. In the twentieth century, women began to emerge in ministry and leadership roles, first in the holiness churches and then with the Pentecostals. The examples are numerous, the most notable being Aimee Semple McPherson, the founder of the International Church of the Four Square Gospel, and Kathryn Kuhlmann. David Yonggi Cho has released women into ministry and leadership positions in the Full Gospel Central Church in Seoul, South Korea, and with their help has built the world's largest church with over half a million members.

Women's ministry at Metro Vineyard

We have had a number of women in our midst who have made some profound, accurate and edifying contributions to our prophetic ministry and we are enthusiastic about women moving in the prophetic arena. The limits and extent of a woman's function on the prophetic team at Metro Vineyard Fellowship is the same as that of a man. We no longer give prophetic people a prominent public platform—men or women. Paul Cain, whom we regard very highly, speaks to our church about two or three times a year. However, he gives most of what he receives for us to our main leadership group, either in person or by telephone. Nevertheless, if a woman has the same level of prophetic revelation that Paul Cain has, she will be given the same honour and platform as he is, whether that platform be public or communicating with our main leadership group. Any woman preacher who has the anointing to teach will be given some opportunity based on her proven teaching gift. Over the years, we have had several woman preachers speak to our whole church when we've discerned in them the gifting to preach.

We have identified a prophetic network of about seventy people at Metro Vineyard Fellowship who regularly receive dreams, visions and prophetic words from the Lord. They meet periodically with Michael as the leader. Michael also gives pastoral oversight to the itinerant ministries and the established prophetic ministries in our church. There is a prophetic council made up of about a dozen people, several of whom are women. This council leads the larger prophetic network. They help nurture these people in their gifting, listen to their prophetic revelation and help them with the interpretation and application. This prophetic fellowship legitimises what they are doing and provides a place for encouragement, correction and judgement within a community of people who have the same type of giftings. They feel free to express themselves in a friendly atmosphere where they can receive both direction and correction.

Stereotypical women

Stereotypes, prejudices and unfair biases are commonly directed against women. It is a powerful reality throughout the Western world that hinders the work of God. It exists in our church as well and is something we strongly address on proper occasions.

Our deeply embedded stereotypes primarily come from our culture. It is even more pronounced in the American Bible-belt where a woman's place is in the home, and her place in church is to be quiet. We realise the vast importance of a woman's impact on the present and future generation, and we therefore highly honour and esteem the ministry of a mother in the home. But we do believe that women are often called to function outside the home as they serve the kingdom of God.

There are also stereotypes about women and their psychological make-up, most commonly that they are very intuitive, but without the proper restraint to control the emotional side of their nature. I don't think it is a fair stereotype. I believe some women certainly can be described that way, but some men are like that as well. I think it is too generalised a stereotype and should not be the key used to hinder women from ministry. Both men and women are intuitive, but my experience is that there are more women who have a stronger intuitive part of their nature than do men. A man's stereotype is that he is always in control, but out of touch with his and other people's feelings. That's not always true either.

Dysfunctional relational skills among men and women have always caused many problems both in society and in the church. Some men have unfounded fears about women in ministry and are afraid to allow women to prophesy or to preach. The problem is exacerbated by some of the radical feminist movements that are so publicised today. Consequently, some men tend to dig in their heels and resist valid biblical expressions of women in ministry. I do believe that if the men had been honouring women in the church all along, it might have diffused some of the radical feminist movements in our society. If the church had been leading the way by honouring women in the church, it might have had an impact on the entire society. If there had been more women prominent in society because of the strength of affirmation by men in the church, the negative effects of the radical feminist movement could have been minimised. This is one practical way in which the church functions as a prophetic standard-bearer to society; that is, by honouring both women and children in a way befitting the grace of God (Mal 4:6; 1 Pet 3:7).

The Jezebel spirit

One of the most misunderstood issues relating to prophetic women in the church is the idea of a 'Jezebel spirit', particularly when the term is defined as: a controlling woman who dominates men. We understand that there is no precise biblical term called the 'Jezebel spirit'. However, there is a powerfully negative 'Jezebel-type spirit' or attitude in which some people seem to be immersed. When a woman stands up to a man and confronts him in any way, even if the man has major problems with insecurity and leadership ability, sometimes the woman is quickly referred to as having a 'Jezebel spirit'. Some women do have an inappropriate, domineering spirit. Some men in the church have an identical problem! Too many women who have a legitimate leadership gift are labelled 'Jezebel', simply because they clash with a man who has a controlling personality. Sometimes these women are a little wounded. Perhaps their social and relational skills need refining, but men need improvement in their social skills too, especially those who are insecure and try to manipulate women. Some women simply won't allow such men to dominate and hinder their place of service in God's kingdom. These women can really suffer from unrighteous judgements against them because they simply spoke up and challenged a man who had a wrong spirit. This does not make them a 'Jezebel'.

It trips a wire in my own soul when I hear a woman quickly written off as a 'Jezebel'. It can be a crushing emotional blow to a woman. It is usually an unfair judgement that can unjustly cause her to repress or neglect her ministry gift for years.

I believe that both domineering women and dominating men need to be confronted and then hindered from having too much influence in the church. But when some leaders see domineering men they tend to wink at the problem and say, 'Well, you know he has a strong personality and that's just the way he is.'

But when women act in the same way, all kinds of unjust spiritual implications become attached to it.

Jezebel—seduction to immorality

I believe the idea of a 'Jezebel spirit' *does* involve an element of domination and control. Between Queen Jezebel and King Ahab, Jezebel clearly seemed to be the more dominant (1 Kings 18). However, Jesus defined a 'Jezebel-type spirit' very specifically in terms other than domination. Jesus said, 'You allow that woman Jezebel, who calls herself a prophetess, to teach and seduce My servants to commit sexual immorality' (Rev 2:20). A 'Jezebel-type spirit' then can be described as one who leads the people of God to embrace immorality in a carefree way. This primarily refers to someone with a 'seducing spirit'.

When we talk about being seduced these days, we tend to think of it as something women do to men. But some strong male leaders, even within the body of Christ, have a potential to seduce women. They can have a powerful sensual or emotional impact on women. In this way, men can be as seductive as women. Consequently, a man can be likened to Jezebel.

I think the most seductive 'Jezebel-type spirit' in the world today is found in certain aspects of the media industry, which is very effective in desensitising and beguiling the nations to commit acts of immorality. They have promoted the prostitution racket and the 18-rated film industry. They are the ones who perpetuate the stereotype of the woman as the seductress, but it is really their love of money that pours the fuel on the fire of seduction in our society. They, more than anyone, have the characteristics of Jezebel.

If women should get a break anywhere, it should be in the church.

The prejudice towards women is often due to dysfunctional relational skills that exist with both men and women. In these negative situations, the pastors are sometimes called controlling by the women and the women are sometimes called 'Jezebels' by the pastors. This is all ridiculous. What needs to be done is for both the men and the women to be healed. We need to esteem and make room for women with valid leadership gifts in the church. Some pastors need to be less defensive and insecure in their leadership style. We need to replace the harsh judgements between men and women with the honour and patience that Jesus lavishes upon each of us who are still immature in our character, wisdom and gifting.

Acts 2:17–18 says that God shall pour out his Spirit on his sons *and daughters*, and they shall prophesy. The church in the end times will flourish as both men and women receive powerful dreams and visions that bring others to deep relationships with Jesus. We will never be fully effective if one half of God's army is kept out of the battle against Satan's onslaught. We need the men and women both to take their place boldly together before God's throne and to function with confidence and security together in the body of Christ. Together we can experience the passionate love of God for us and then use our authority in Jesus to plunder the kingdom of darkness in our generation effectively.

15

Eight Dimensions of the Prophetic Church

The term 'prophetic' is used by some in the church to refer either to the fulfilment of end-time events or the speaking forth of revelatory messages. The New Testament church is to be a prophetic servant community, not only in these areas, but in a much broader and multi-dimensional way. To be prophetic is not simply something 'charismatics' do, but it is essential to the very nature and mission of the entire body of Christ on earth.

Those involved in prophetic ministry need to see what they are doing in the larger context of all the other dimensions of the church's calling as a prophetic servant community. People who receive dreams and visions do not comprise *the* prophetic ministry in its entirety, but are really only one expression of a community that is prophetic in at least eight dimensions.

Some of these eight categories or dimensions of prophetic expression may overlap in the same way as do the gifts of the Spirit. The list of the nine gifts of the Spirit (1 Cor 12:7–11) is simply a description of how the person of the Holy Spirit moves through individuals in the church. Sometimes it is hard to categorise and define certain manifestations. Was it a word of wisdom, a prophecy or the discerning of spirits? In the same way these eight dimensions of the church as a prophetic servant community may overlap in some aspects. The point is that prophetic ministry is not just something the church *does*, but something it *is* by its very nature.

1. Revealing the heart of God

The angel of God told the Apostle John that the testimony of Jesus is the spirit of prophecy (Rev 19:10). The fresh revelation of Jesus' heart is the essence of his testimony. This includes the revealing of who he is, along with what he does and how he feels. The spirit of prophecy which speaks of the purpose of prophecy is to reveal these aspects of Jesus' testimony. Passion for Jesus is the result of this prophetic revelation. Such holy passion is the highlight of the prophetic church.

The prophetic ministry is to be stamped and sealed with an affection for and sensitivity to the heart of God. It is a ministry that passionately *feels* and *reveals* the divine heart to the church and the world. Prophetic ministry has to do not only with information but, in the first order, the ability to experience in some measure the compassion, grief and joy of God, and then a passion for God. Then out of that experience of God will come the revelation of some of his future plans and purposes. If you 'desire earnestly to prophesy' (1 Cor 14:39) by merely seeking information from the *mind* of God, you have by-passed the cornerstone and essence of prophetic ministry—that is, the revelation of his *heart*. The Apostle Paul said, 'Though I have the gift of prophecy and understand all mysteries and all knowledge . . . but have not love [for God and people], I am nothing' (1 Cor 13:2). Prophets in the Old Testament often prefaced their message and ministry by declaring, 'The burden of the Lord which came. . .' (eg Hab 1:1).

So then, one prophetic dimension of the church's ministry is to proclaim, reveal and call to remembrance the intimacies and affections of God. That includes, of course, his jealous longing over his people, his magnificent compassion and his intense grief over our sin that separates us from him.

The outcome of this revealing of God's heart is the stirring of people's passion for God. The response to such great love is to worship him and love him in return. Many at Metro Vineyard have been used splendidly as prophetic worship leaders who have fanned the flames of people's spiritual passions through worship. Through worship tapes and leading worship at conferences, these prophetic men have been the source of refreshing for many. The revealing and stirring through anointed music is fulfilling a prophetic dimension of the church.

My favourite message is that our passionate affection for Jesus is the result of an ever-increasing revelation of the loveliness of his personality that is filled with passion for us. Though I rarely voice a prophetic word in the church, I seek to contribute to the mission of the church as a prophetic servant community by teaching on the passionate heart of God.

2. The fulfilment of biblical prophecy

For thousands of years the prophets foretold of the Messiah who was to come, and of the kingdom that he would establish. Jesus spoke of it sometimes in the sense that the kingdom had come with the advent of his public ministry and at other times as if the kingdom was 'not yet'. In whatever sense and to whatever extent the kingdom *has* come, those to whom it has come are the living fulfilment of what the prophets had spoken.

Jesus said to Peter, 'On this rock I will build My church, and the gates of Hades shall not prevail against it' (Mt 16:18). Throughout the last two millennia all the powers of hell have been unable to withstand the gospel or the church. It has only continued to grow. Jesus described the expanding kingdom of God like this: 'It is like a mustard seed which, when it is sown on the ground, is smaller than all the seeds on earth; but when it is sown, it grows up and becomes greater than all herbs, and shoots out large branches, so that the birds of the air may nest under its shade' (Mk 4:31–32).

The church in its survival and growth is living out the prophetic word. It is in its very presence a continuing witness to prophecies fulfilled.

The church is also a prophetic witness in its mission. Just as the apostles in the early days, the church today is *the* witness to the death and resurrection of Jesus Christ. Its primary task has always been to preserve and proclaim what God has said, the good news of his death, resurrection and his coming again to judge the world. The church is both a living testimony of prophecy fulfilled and a prophetic voice of what will come in the future. By this the church functions as the salt of the earth that restrains it from plunging headlong into corruption.

As the bride of Christ, all that the church does in order to make herself ready (Eph 5:27) is a prophetic trumpet to the world of the relationship of Christ to the church and to the fact that Christ is coming again. The next time you are sitting in a church service, remember that even though we are almost 2,000 years removed from the first-century church, nevertheless, the very fact that you are there gathering in his name is both a prophetic fulfilment and a prophetic statement to the world.

3. The prophetic standard in the Scriptures

One of the most vital prophetic realities is the Scriptures themselves. They are a trumpet of God's heart, purpose and will. How precious to the body of Christ is the fact that God gave us the Scriptures.

For each of the eight prophetic dimensions of the church, God raises up leaders who are both equipped by the Holy Spirit and have worked hard to equip themselves. For us at Metro

Vineyard, certain people have made a vital contribution over the years within the context of our prophetic community. They have extensive seminary degrees and are experts in exegesis, hermeneutics, systematic theology and the history of the church. Prophets and exhorters among us sometimes want to interpret or apply a scripture in a particular way because it proves a point or simply because it 'preaches well'. For them these 'doctors of the word' serve as a balance and a plumbline.

People with a thorough understanding of the historical context of the New Testament writings (to whom they were written and why), as well as the extra-biblical tradition of the second- and third-century church fathers (their historical recollections), play an essential role in kindling the church's self-awareness as a prophetic community. The New Testament epistles were not written like lessons for a Sunday school curriculum. They were letters to people like us who were at times going through very difficult situations. When we as a church hear about the conflicts that caused the writings of 2 Corinthians, or the drama which is the background of the letter to the Hebrews, we begin to identify with the *people* of the New Testament, not just with the exhortations to them. Not only does this make the New Testament come alive, but it gives the church a sense of connection with those who began the race.

The church as a prophetic community must realise that we are a continuation of what they began. We must feel that connectedness. The torch has been passed so many times, it is easy to lose sight of the fact that we are running the same race they started. Their leg of the race has been completed, and they have now gathered at the finish line to cheer us on. The church is the living testimony of the prophetic purpose of God in history. It is also a prophetic community that is to preserve and proclaim accurately the word of God.

4. Moving when the cloud moves

The fourth way in which the church must be prophetic is that it must discern the current move of the Spirit; the 'present truth' as Dick Iverson calls it. Just as the Children of Israel followed the cloud through the wilderness, the church needs to move when the Holy Spirit says to move (Deut 1:33). This is in contrast to the aspect of the prophetic community we have just discussed. While the truth that the church preserves and proclaims from the Scriptures is unchangeable and immovable, it is not a static relationship that exists between the church and the Holy Spirit. The Spirit is constantly doing a new thing with the church as a whole and, separately, with each congregation.

The kind of moving I am referring to is the changing emphasis placed on elements of truth, structure and strategy. We are so to speak, moving around within the boundaries of the unchangeable truth of God's word. Some recent examples of people sensing the Lord's wisdom and instruction concerning the means and methods of the church's prophetic expression are:

(a) The current emphasis on small group or cell-based churches;

(b) The emphasis on the public expression of worship beginning in England with Roger Forster, Graham Kendrick, Lynn Green and Gerald Coates. Today that movement which began as a small public gathering is known and practised worldwide as March for Jesus;

(c) The refreshing of the Holy Spirit as experienced in charismatic churches around the world;

(d) The current movement towards prayer that has been spear-headed by people like C. Peter Wagner, Dick Eastman, Wesley Tullis and Larry Lea.

Again, the leaders of such movements are not necessarily those who exercise the 'gift of prophecy' as mentioned in

1 Corinthians 12, but are people who can clearly sense the direction in which the 'cloud' is moving. They might be compared to the sons of Issachar who 'had understanding of the times, to know what Israel ought to do' (1 Chron 12:32). There is nothing more prophetic than the church of Jesus Christ 'following the cloud'; that is, the current emphasis and leading of the Holy Spirit. This is a prophetic dimension that can be entirely distinct from dreams, visions or the manifestation of the gift of prophecy. It is an expression of prophetic leadership.

There are a lot of people who proclaim that they know exactly what the Holy Spirit is saying to the church, many of whom are saying opposite things. But it is when *the people* sense the witness of the Holy Spirit in that proclamation that the benefit begins. Those prophetic-type leaders who accurately discern the 'movement of the cloud' are essential to the church. The church's history is filled with examples of how part of the body of Christ discerned the present emphasis of the Holy Spirit as it related to the structure, strategy or particular elements of truth. However, some have 'followed the cloud' to the next place in God and then never moved again. After camping around a certain structure, strategy or truth for a period of time, they can become less of a prophetic community and more of a prophetic monument to something the Holy Spirit did long ago. That doesn't mean we should abandon all the older traditions with every new 'move of the cloud'. The greatest expression of the church as a prophetic community is in those congregations or denominations which 'move on with the cloud', but carry all the wisdom, experience and maturity of their history with them.

5. Demonstrating the power of God

Elijah was a prophet of God who called down fire from heaven as a sign of God's power. In the New Testament, attesting miracles are not limited to the prophets. The Holy Spirit distributes the gifts 'individually as he wills', one of those being the gift of the working of miracles (1 Cor 12:10–11). Nevertheless, in a general sense the demonstration of the supernatural power of God in and through the church is a dimension of the prophetic ministry.

As in the days of Elijah, miracles attest to the truth of God's word. Some have said that the church doesn't need the miraculous today since we have the written word. But the written word includes the witness of the apostles, and if attesting miracles were needed when they personally testified within a few years of the resurrection, how much more are attesting miracles needed today to confirm the veracity of their written accounts!

Attesting miracles are also valuable as a dimension of the prophetic community because, more than anything else, they make people aware that God is actually present with them. The death and resurrection of Jesus, by the way we estimate time, was very long ago. Without a renewed awareness of his presence, the church sometimes begins to take on the air of a society gathered to venerate the memory of Jesus who 'died 2,000 years ago'. The working of miracles jolts our sensibilities and makes us joyfully—or frightfully—aware of the fact that he is in our midst by the presence of the Holy Spirit, and he is very close to each one of us. A hundred sermons on God being with us may not awaken our hearts as much as a personal encounter of the manifestation of his presence and power through the miraculous. This in no way diminishes the power or authority of the written word. It simply means that in the miraculous, the living God of the written word 'shows up' in a powerfully personal, intimate and tangible way. Through the miraculous, the church prophesies and proclaims that he is alive!

6. Prophetic dreams and visions

The majority of this book is concerned with the nurturing and administrating of the prophetic ministry as it receives revelation from God. God raises up and endows people with gifts to see and hear things that most people do not see or hear. The term 'seer' carries with it some very negative connotations because of its modern-day, non-Christian applications. Consequently, if ever referring to someone as a 'seer', one must be careful to qualify and define this term in the light of 1 Samuel 9: 'Formerly in Israel, when a man went to inquire of God, he spoke thus: "Come, let us go to the seer"; for he who is now called a prophet was formerly called a seer) . . . Samuel answered Saul and said, "I am the seer"' (1 Sam 9:9, 19).

Often these types of prophetic people are not as gifted with great demonstrations of miraculous power, but they regularly *see* things by the Holy Spirit. They see future events, the secrets of people's hearts, as well as the calling of God and destinies on people's lives. Ezekiel was a person who regularly saw things, and like Ezekiel's visions, the things people see today are sometimes as baffling. Nevertheless, the prophetic ministry has been a part of the New Testament from the very beginning.

Prophets like Ezekiel and Zechariah, who are known for seeing profound visions of God, are not known for demonstrations of power like healing the sick or raising the dead.

7. Crying out against social injustice

The church has the responsibility to be a 'prophet to the nation' concerning injustice, repression and the unrighteousness that eventually cause a nation to provoke the judgement of God. One of the more outstanding examples of this was the prophetic outcry from the Revd William Wilberforce working within the church, and Lord Shaftesbury crying out in the British House of Lords. Between these two men, denouncing injustice on two different fronts, they almost singlehandedly caused the British Parliament to outlaw the trading of slaves in England.

Many times prophets to the nation speak from a secular platform and not necessarily as those who represent the church. Joseph and Daniel were two biblical examples of people who represented God in a position of secular power. Abraham Lincoln and Martin Luther King prophetically stood for justice and righteousness in our social order. They were not seen as prophetic from the traditional position of being on a church staff.

The church must be careful not to undermine its prophetic ministry to the nation. Hopefully, many members of the church will be actively involved in civil government and even in party politics. However, the church and those who speak for the church *must* understand where to draw the line. When they enter politics, they do so as godly individuals, not as members of the pastoral staff who are financed by the local church. It is my conviction that the church as an institution should be as a prophet standing for the advancement of righteousness without indebtedness to political party affiliations.

8. Crying out for personal holiness and repentance

John Wesley turned England back to God when the people's personal unrighteousness and apathy had brought them to the edge of societal chaos. God has raised up leaders in the church throughout the generations who have functioned as prophets of God crying against the sins of the people. This is similar to the prophetic cry against social injustice, but different in that the address is specifically to the people in the church. It is less like Jonah prophesying against Nineveh and more like Isaiah and Jeremiah prophesying to Israel and Judah. People like Billy Graham, Charles Colson, John Piper, David Wilkerson and A. W. Tozer stand out in my mind as prophetic ministers raised up to cry out against unrighteousness in the church as they reveal the deep things about the knowledge of God. Their words are anointed by the Spirit to awaken hearts to holiness and passion for Jesus. God uses such prophetic voices like John the Baptist to prick the consciences of believers unto full revival.

Serving in the prophetic community

It is the nature of the church to be the prophetic expression of the kingdom of God on earth; to represent, preserve and proclaim the truth of God to this world. All the members who serve the church or function as a ministry of the church are themselves involved with the ongoing prophetic plan and purpose of God in the earth. Those particularly gifted with dreams, visions, prophecies and revelation need to be careful not to think of themselves too highly—as being *the* prophetic group. They serve only one dimension of the church's greater calling as a prophetic community.

Appendix I

'God's Manifest Presence'

by
Mike Bickle & Michael Sullivant

Understanding the phenomena that accompany the Holy Spirit's ministry

1. Introduction

When God chooses to show his power in and through the body of Christ, opportunities are provided for both tremendous spiritual growth and tragic confusion and stumbling. Throughout both biblical and church history strange and even bizarre physical phenomena have accompanied outpourings of the Holy Spirit's power. In this season, there are numerous reports of widespread occurrences of the manifestations of the Spirit across many parts of the world. Many believers are being blessed, refreshed and rejuvenated. Other believers are not so blessed! They are sceptical and questioning whether thesekinds of things can actually represent a genuine work of God. And what about the obvious fleshly behaviour in which some engage

---

This article on the present manifestations of the holy spirit is based on a booklet available through our Abounding Grace Bookstore. To order, call 001–816–763–3070, or our toll free number in the USA only 1–9000–552–2449, or write to: Abounding Grace Bookstore, PO Box 229, Grandview, MO 64030, or fax 001–816–761–9560.

and try to blame on the Spirit? What shall we do with that? We present this simple outline to the body of Christ in the hope that it will help provide for some a philosophical/theological framework through which these physical phenomena may be viewed and interpreted.

2. Biblical precedents for the manifestations

(a) The Bible does not record all the possible legitimate supernatural experiences. Rather it records examples of legitimate supernatural experiences that fall into broader categories that are typical of how the Holy Spirit works. This concept is taught in John 21:25 in which John states that if all the works that Jesus did had been recorded, all the books in the world could not contain them! God is always and for ever free to do unprecedented things that are consistent with his character and the principles of Scripture.

(b) Somtimes people stretch scripture to try to prove validity of some manifestation that is not explicitly referred to in the Bible. (For example, trying to find proof texts for uncontrollable laughing, yet it is not specifically mentioned in scripture. However, 'joy unspeakable and full of glory' is!

(c) To test the validity of a manifestation we should look at the overall beliefs and lifestyles (and changes in them!) of those affected, the overall beliefs and lifestyles of those being used to impart the experience, the short- and long-term 'fruit' of the experience, and the overall glory given to Jesus Christ in the general context in which the manifestations are occurring. Jonathan Edwards referred to five tests to determine if a manifestation is a true work of the Holy Spirit. He states that Satan cannot—and would not if he could—generate these kinds of things in people. If we can answer 'yes' to one or more of these questions, then it is to be regarded as genuine, despite any 'little objections, as many [people] make from oddities, irregularities, errors in conduct, and the delusions and scandals of some professors [people who claim to be believers]', ie some 'human mixture' does not invalidate a general work of true revival—in fact, some should be expected.

(i) Does it bring honour to the person of Jesus Christ?
(ii) Does it produce a greater hatred of sin and a greater love for righteousness?
(iii) Does it produce a greater regard for Scripture?
(iv) Does it lead people into truth?
(v) Does it produce a greater love for God and man?

(d) The basis for the occurrence of physical manifestations is rooted in the biblical doctrine of the 'manifest presence' of God.

(i) Contrasted with the 'omnipresence' of God—ie God is everywhere, but he also reveals his powerful presence at specific times, in particular places and for various reasons.
(ii) God 'comes down' and interfaces with the natural realm
(iii) When the omnipotent, omniscient, omnipresent, eternal, infinite, holy, just and loving God condescends to 'come down' and touch weak and finite humans, what would you expect or predict might happen to the natural and normal order of things?

(e) A few biblical examples of the 'manifest presence' of God:

- John 18:6—Unbelieving guards thrown to the ground.
- Acts 9:4—Saul of Tarsus sees brilliant light, thrown from his horse, hears Jesus audibly, is temporarily struck blind.
- Revelation 1:17—John falls as dead, has no bodily strength, and sees and hears into the spirit world.
- Daniel 8:17; 10:7–10, 15–19—Daniel falls, has no

strength, terrified by God's presence.

- 1 Kings 8:10–11—The priests can't stand because of God's glory.
- 2 Chronicles 7:1–3—Solomon and priests can't stand because of God's glory.
- Acts 10:10; 22:1—Peter and Paul fall into trances and see and hear into the spirit world.
- 1 Samuel 19:18–24—King Saul and his antagonistic men are overcome by the Holy Spirit and prophesy as they near the camp of the prophets.
- Exodus 19:16f.—Thunder, smoke, shaking of the ground, sounds of trumpets and voices upon Mount Sinai.
- Exodus 34:30f.—Moses' face supernaturally shines.
- Matthew 17:2–8—Jesus and his garment supernaturally made brilliant, a supernatural cloud, accompanied by Moses and Elijah.
- Exodus 3:2—Bush is burning, but not consumed.
- John 1:32—The Holy Spirit descends in visible form as a dove.
- Leviticus 9:24; 1 Kings 18:38; 1 Chronicles 21:26—Fire from heaven consumes sacrifices.
- 2 Corinthians 5:12–13—Paul describes being 'beside himself' as opposed to being sober.
- Luke 2:35—A virgin conceives the Son of God.

3. Historical precedents for the manifestations

Extraordinary physical phenomena caused by the operation of the Holy Spirit's presence upon people is fully documented and affirmed throughout the history of revivals in virtually every branch of the Christian church. Following are just several of hundreds of possible quotations substantiating this fact.

(a) St Teresa of Avila (1515–1582) on being 'rapt in ecstasy':

The subject rarely loses consciousness; I have sometimes lost it altogether, but only seldom and for but a short time. As a rule the consciousness is disturbed; and though incapable of action with respect to outward things, the subject can still hear and understand, but only dimly, as though from a long way off.[1]

(b) Jonathan Edwards, regarded to be one of the greatest theologians of history, lived during the time of the Great Awakening in America in the 1730s and 1740s. Edwards provides the most thoughtful and comprehensive biblical evaluations, reflections and writings about the manifestations of the Spirit.

It was very wonderful to see how persons' affections were sometimes moved—when God did as it were suddenly open their eyes, and let into their minds a sense of the greatness of his grace, the fullness of Christ, and his readiness to save . . . Their joyful surprise has caused their hearts as it were to leap, so that they have been ready to break forth into laughter, tears often at the same time issuing like a flood, and intermingling a loud weeping. Sometimes they have not been able to forbear crying out with a loud voice, expressing their great admiration.[1]

. . .some persons having had such longing desires after Christ or which have risen to such degree, as to take away their natural strength. Some have been so overcome with a sense of the dying love of Christ to such poor, wretched, and unworthy creatures, as to weaken the body. Several persons have had so great a sense of the glory of God, and excellency of Christ, that nature and life seemed almost to sink under it; and in all probability, if God had showed them a little more of

[1] Francis MacNutt, *Overcome by the Spirit* (Chosen Books, 1990).
[2] 'A Narrative of Surprising Conversions', *The Works of Edwards* (vol. 4), pp. 37–38.

himself, it would have dissolved their frame . . . And they have talked, when able to speak, of the glory of God's perfections.[1]

It was a very frequent thing to see a house full of outcries, faintings, convulsions and such like, both with distress, and also with admiration and joy.[2]

Many in their religious affections being raised far beyond what they ever had been before: and there were some instances of persons lying in a sort of trance, remaining for perhaps a whole twenty-four hours motionless, and with their senses locked up; but in the meantime under strong imagination, as though they went to heaven, and had there a vision of glorious and delightful objects.[3]

(c) The following was the report of an atheist 'free thinker' named James B. Finley, who attended the Cane Ridge, Kentucky revival in 1801:

The noise was like the roar of Niagara. The vast sea of human beings seemed to be agitated as if by a storm . . . Some of the people were singing, others praying, some crying for mercy in the most piteous accents, while others were shouting vociferously. While witnessing these scenes, a peculiarly-strange sensation, such as I had never felt before, came over me. My heart beat tumultuously, my knees trembled, my lip quivered, and I felt as though I must fall to the ground. A strange supernatural power seemed to pervade the entire mass of mind there collected . . . At one time I saw at least five hundred, swept down in a moment as if a battery of a thousand guns had been opened upon them, and then immediately followed shrieks and shouts that rent the very heavens . . . I fled for the woods a second time, and wished I had stayed at home.[4]

---

[1] 'A Narrative of Surprising Conversions', *The Works of Edwards* (vol. 4), p. 45.
[2] 'The Great Awakening', *The Works of Edwards* (vol. 4), p. 547
3 Ibid, p. 550.
[4] John White, *When the Spirit Comes with Power*, p. 70.

4. Catalogue of manifestations

The Hebrew and biblical model of the unity of personality implies that the spirit affects the body. At times the human spirit is so affected by the glory of God, the human body is not capable of containing the intensity of these spiritual encounters, and strange physical behaviour results. Sometimes, though certainly not always, the bodily responses are human responses to the spirit's activity and not directly caused by the Holy Spirit. However, this does not imply that they are therefore carnal and should be forbidden. Following are phenomena that have been observed in contemporary experience: shaking, jerking, loss of bodily strength, heavy breathing, eyes fluttering, lips trembling, oil on the body, changes in skin colour, weeping, laughing, intoxication ('drunkenness'), staggering, travailing, dancing, falling, visions, hearing audibly into the spirit realm, inspired utterances (ie prophecy, tongues, interpretation), angelic visitations and manifestations, jumping, violent rolling, screaming, wind, heat, electricity, coldness, nausea as discernment of evil, smelling or tasting good or evil presences, tingling, pain in the body as discernment of illnesses, feeling heavy weight or lightness, trances (altered physical state while seeing and hearing into the spirit world), inability to speak normally; and disruption of the natural realm (eg electrical circuits blown).

5. Purposes for the manifestations

(a) God often chooses foolish things to accomplish his work (1 Cor 1:27–28). He offends the mind to test the heart. In the account of the outpouring of the Spirit at Pentecost in Acts 2:12–13, some people were amazed, some were perplexed and some mocked. We continue to see these three responses to the work of the Spirit today. This 'way of God' challenges our improper 'control issues' and breaks down our unsanctified inhibitions and pride.

(b) The demonstration of God's power through signs and wonders—signs point to the God who is beyond them; wonders cause intrigue concerning the mystery of God's ways. God wants our faith to rest upon his power and not the wisdom of men's words (1 Cor 2:4–5).

(c) Experiential intimacy with God—knowing God and being known by him.

(d) Grace and power to overcome inner bondages—fear, lust, pride, envy, greed, deceit, bitterness, etc.

(e) Impartations of love, peace, joy, fear of God, etc.

(f) Healings—physical and emotional.

(g) Bonding experiences with other believers—relational barriers fall when people experience the Spirit's presence together.

(h) Empowering for ministering to others—anointing for service.

(i) Release of God's word—prophetic sensitising, powerful preaching.

(j) Intercession—apprehended for effective, Spirit-led prayer.

(k) Enlarging and liberating of spiritual capacities.

(l) The manifestations are given for refreshment, encouragement and healing. This should lead to deeper discipleship (growth in faith, hope and love). This should then lead to effective evangelism and, hopefully, full revival.

6. Exposing false equations about the manifestations

(a) 'If I were more devoted, then I would experience these manifestations of the Spirit.' The experience of these things is not related to our spiritual passion and diligence, but is the operation of the grace and providence of God.

(b) 'Many people were visibly touched by the Holy Spirit. Revival is here!' Actually the classical understanding of revival goes far beyond the experience of manifestations to deep and far-reaching spiritual and practical transformations of individuals, spiritual movements, geographic regions and whole nations.

The terms 'refreshing' and 'renewal' are more appropriate for the present work of the Spirit. Hopefully it will lead to full revival. All the more, then, let us keep praying and believing for it!

(c) 'Those people God is using to impart his power are really mature and sensitive to God. God must really love them a lot more than he does me. But if I'm diligent enough, maybe I'll become qualified to do those same things.' People who have moved in 'power ministry' have often unwittingly conveyed the notion that the power gifts are merit badges of spirituality. This has brought many dedicated and sincere believers into condemnation. These gifts and callings are free gifts of grace and God gives them as he wills to various members of the body of Christ. In times of spiritual visitation more members than normal are used to impart the Holy Spirit.

(d) 'Just be open and sensitive to the Holy Spirit and you will be touched too.' It would be far less perplexing if this was the way it worked, but it isn't. Although people may have emotional barriers that hinder the work of the Spirit, many who are sceptical and cynical have been powerfully and visibly touched by God. Others who are very open and hungry for a touch are not powerfully affected, at least not outwardly. We must refrain from judging who is 'open' and who is 'closed' as assuming this may be aiding or hindering a person from receiving from God. If you believe you may have such a barrier, ask God to reveal the nature of it to you. He will be faithful, in his time, to answer such a request. In the meantime, do not assume that it must be a barrier that is keeping you from receiving from God.

(e) 'If it is truly the Holy Spirit touching and moving upon these people, then there will be instant and/or lasting "fruit" in their lives.' Actually, God moves upon and woos many people closer to himself who never bring forth the fruit that he intends through these encounters with his grace. There are no guarantees that 'fruit' will result from these 'divine invitations'. People are free to respond fully or partially, or even to ignore such spiritual opportunities.

(f) 'If it is really the power of the Holy Spirit on these people, then they should not have any control over their responses and behaviour.' There are such things as 'uncontrollable' experiences with the Spirit; however, these are actually more uncommon than many people think. There is a mysterious combination of the divine and human powers surrounding the Spirit's work. Peter knew how to walk and had the power to do so when Jesus invited him out onto the water. The supernatural side of the event was that he didn't sink as he walked. On the front end of welcoming the Spirit's manifest presence, there is more control at our disposal to respond to his activity. In the middle of a welcomed experience with the Spirit, there is typically less control on the human side, but even still, there remains an ability to 'pull out' of the experience if the need or desire is present. There are exceptions to this general rule and we must learn to recognise them. 'There is a time for everything,' said Solomon. The Holy Spirit knows this (he wrote it!), and he is not necessarily quenched when those in authority in the church or a given meeting discern, for instance, that the time for quiet, attentive listening to the preaching of the Scripture has come and they therefore ask the assembly to respond accordingly. This is not automatically to be considered the manifestation of a 'control spirit'! Loving community implies individual restraint. Absolute freedom is absolute nonsense!

7. Exposing dangers regarding the manifestations

(a) Possibility of divisions and judgements within the body— we must seek to avoid the 'haves' and 'have nots' mentality at all costs. This will truly grieve the Spirit of God (see Rom 14 and 1 Cor 12–14). Love for God and one another must remain the pre-eminent value of Christian community.

(b) Fanaticism—in their enthusiasm, people can get carried

away into excesses of behaviour and be deluded into embracing strange and unbiblical ideas. This problem must be addressed as it arises. We should seek to do this with compassion, both privately and publicly. This is a very delicate procedure, for the true fire of the Spirit will always be attended by a measure of 'wildfire' introduced by the fleshly elements still resident within imperfect believers.

(c) Neglect of the less intoxicating and less noticeable aspects of our faith—things such as daily devotions, secret prayer, humble service, helping the poor, showing mercy, loving enemies, suffering patiently, honouring parents and other authorities, restraining appetites, training children, working hard, doing chores and errands, paying tithes, bills and taxes, resolving relational conflicts, and being faithful friends.

(d) Casting off all restraints and disciplines in the name of 'the liberty of the Spirit'. This tension between liberty and restraint must be embraced by the whole church. We will not always agree with how this tension is stewarded by the members of the body. Be prepared to 'swallow some gnats' to avoid 'swallowing camels'!

(e) Becoming distracted from focusing on God and other present purposes (ie passion for Jesus, small groups, community, intercession, evangelism) by undue time, fascination and attention given to the manifestations themselves.

(f) Falling into the pride of grace—there is no uglier form of pride than the arrogant boastings or subtle self-righteousness of people who have been blessed by the Spirit. These graces are dispensed to magnify the grace and mercy of God and lead us into gratitude and humility. If we do not humble ourselves, God, in his love, will at some point allow us to be humiliated.

(g) Spreading of rumours and misinformation—although some of this is unavoidable, with good communication and proper qualifiers it can be reduced. Take no delight in and work at doubting bad reports!

(h) Exalting outward manifestations above the inward and

hidden work of the Spirit within people's hearts. Progressive internal transformation into the image of Jesus is the ultimate goal of the Spirit's work.

(i) Exalting the weak human instruments that God is especially using as catalysts in the work of the Spirit—we must avoid any kind of 'hero worship' within our hearts. However, the 'facelessness' of God's army does not mean that there will not be any visible leaders or prominent members with public ministries within the body. It refers to the attitude of humility, submission and deference that all the members and leaders embrace within their hearts.

8. Proper responses to the manifestations

(a) Taking the posture of being 'learners' rather than 'experts' in the ministry of the Spirit.

(b) Being gracious, kind and patient with differences in perspectives within the community of believers.

(c) Giving proper liberty and creating sufficient opportunities for the Spirit to manifest himself.

(d) Encouraging proper restraints—we are appealing for sensitivity to the situation and context. What does love 'look like' or require in this particular setting? Seek to submit to those in authority for the sake of peace and unity. Appeal to them in private if you disagree with the direction they gave or are giving to the body.

(e) Being open and willing to receive freely from God.

(f) Not striving to 'make something happen'.

(g) Expressing gratitude for the present grace of God.

(h) Taking time to wait and be patient in ministry situations.

(i) Searching the Scriptures.

(j) Studying the history of revivals.

(k) Rejoicing in that whether or not you have personally been manifestly touched by the Spirit, God is visiting the body. Let us not be so individualistically-minded.

Appendix II
MVF Mission Statement

Vision statement

- Calling people into the love of God resulting in passion for Jesus and compassion for people (Eph 3:17–19)

Mission statement

- MVF is called to be a New Testament church that, through experiencing the love of God, is passionate for Jesus and compassionate towards people (Mt 22:37–40)
- We desire to fulfil this calling by functioning as a Prophetic Servant Community that evangelises the lost (Mt 28:19-20)

Essential factors

Passion for Jesus—John 17:26

BRIDE

- Freely receiving God's extravagant affection through the finished work of the cross (Rom 5:6:11)
- Because God first loved us, we desire passionately to love, know and enjoy Jesus (Song 8:6–7)

DISCIPLESHIP
- Equipping and discipling believers to believe and obey the Scriptures fully in the fear of God (Mt 28:19–20)
- Knowing how to control our bodies in moral purity and honour (1 Thess 4:3)

Compassion for people—Mt 9:36–38

KINGDOM
- Actively exercising the authority of Jesus over all the works of darkness as we heal the sick, deliver the oppressed, comfort the broken-hearted, and serve the poor (Lk 4:18; 1 Jn 3:8)

ARMY
- Actively extending the kingdom of God in the home, market-place and abroad through intercession, evangelism, good works, church planting and extravagant giving (Mt 10:8; 11:12)

Prophetic—Acts 2:17–21

EMPOWERED
- Fully embracing the Person, revelation and power of the Holy Spirit (Acts 1:8)
- Seeking to walk and worship in the fullness of the Holy Spirit (Eph 5:18)

RESPONSIVE
- Fully yielding our plans to the present-tense direction of the Lord (Deut 1:33)
- Embracing the scriptural order for the local church as modelled by New Testament church values, practices and principles (Mt 9:17)

Servant community—Acts 2:42–47

FAMILY
- Nurturing a kingdom community of healthy friendships and

loving families through a small group structure (Eph 5:22–6:9; Rom 12:15)

- Seeking to be a friendly church that joyfully welcomes and embraces others in the grace of God (Rom 15:1–7)

BODY

- Seeking to function as a unified body comprised of many diverse members (1 Cor 12)
- Rejoining the generations of young and old (Mal 4:6), helping men and women to function fully in their giftings and cultivating ethnic diversity (1 Cor 12)

Appendix III

Grace Training Center

*A Biblical Foundation for a Lifetime of
Passion, Purity, and Power*

Purpose statement

Grace Training Center is a full-time Bible school based in Metro Vineyard Fellowship of Kansas City. It offers one, two, and three year programmes for full-time and part-time students.

The Grace Training Center, a ministry of Metro Vineyard Fellowship, is committed to both the centrality of Scripture and the power of the Holy Spirit. Our goal is to equip men and women for service in God's kingdom by nurturing a biblical harmony between theological integrity and Spirit-empowered passion for Jesus.

Our School of the Word (Division of Biblical Studies) instructs students in the interpretation of Scripture and the essentials of evangelical theology. The School of the Spirit (Division of Christian Ministries) provides training and experience in the application of biblical truth to life and ministry.

Sam Storms, PhD, President

'Daniel tells us that "the people who know their God will display strength and take action" (11:32). GTC exists for this purpose. Our desire is to impart tomorrow's leaders with fresh

243

power and a new vision through the life-changing knowledge of God.'

Mike Bickle, Director

'Grace Training Center was birthed with a vision to combine serious academic study in the word of God with practical ministry training from humble yet gifted and experienced servants of God. Our desire is that you leave GTC more in love with Jesus and better equipped to serve him through the church.'

John Wimber, Association of Vineyard Churches

'One of the pleasures in a growing movement is the emergence of training opportunities such as that occasioned by the Grace Training Center in Kansas City. I am proud of Sam Storms' and Mike Bickle's leadership in this regard.'

Jack Deere, ThD, Author, Surprised by the Power of the Spirit

'I heartily recommend the Grace Training Center to anyone hungry for more of God's word and the skills to minister in the power of the Holy Spirit. The leadership and faculty at the Training Center are committed to fervent passion for Jesus and compassionate love for his people. Grace Training Center provides a unique opportunity for depth in biblical studies and growth in devotion to God.'

Wayne Grudem, PhD, Trinity Evangelical Divinity School

'I am happy to recommend Grace Training Center to people who are seeking deeper training for ministry but are unable to attend a theological seminary. I am confident that GTC, under the capable leadership of Mike Bickle and Sam Storms, will provide sound training in the Bible and theology, mature instruction in practical ministry skills, and scripturally-guided experience of ministry in the power of the Holy Spirit. GTC would be especially helpful for people who want to combine academic teaching with guided experience in Vineyard-style ministries of healing, prophecy, worship, spiritual warfare, intercession, ministries of compassion, and the use of other spiritual gifts.'

Ten distinctives of Grace Training

(1) Cultivation of a holy passion for God

The Training Center seeks not only to provide a solid foundation based on sound biblical theology and the wisdom of seasoned ministers, but also to impart a passion for intimacy with the Lord as the foundation of all ministry.

(2) Commitment to the word of God

The Scriptures are taught from a scholarly evangelical perspective, but with an emphasis on practical application to ministry. Students in our leadership training programmes all major in the Bible, as it is through God's word that God's servants are fully equipped for every good work (2 Tim 3:17).

(3) Community of believers

We believe training for ministry cannot be divorced from practical commitment to fellowship and ministry in a local church setting. Metro Vineyard Fellowship provides a dynamic and exciting environment for personal spiritual growth and practical ministry experience.

(4) Continual intercession for revival

Metro Vineyard Fellowship maintains a strong commitment to unceasing intercession for the outpouring of the Holy Spirit to revive the church, to change the expression and understanding of Christianity in our generation, and to usher in a great harvest of redeemed souls.

(5) Charismatically gifted ministry

Our faculty is committed to ministry in the power of God's Spirit through all the gifts he graciously bestows. Our Christian Ministries division is called the School of the Spirit because we seek to train people to minister with sensitivity to his guidance and through his anointing rather than in human wisdom and energy.

(6) Cell-group based ministry

Life and ministry at MVF are based on a network of small home gatherings that we call Friendship Groups. We believe this will develop the depths of a caring community and an every-member ministry that will be necessary for the church to fulfil God's purposes in the earth.

(7) Church planting vision

The Vineyard movement is committed to evangelism and church planting at home and abroad. We share that commitment and believe involvement in teams starting new congregations holds great opportunity for the expansion of God's kingdom.

(8) Called to the nations

GTC has been formed to equip people to touch the nations and ultimately to serve as an international training centre to help fulfil Christ's Great Commission to make disciples of all nations.

(9) Context for prophetic nurture

MVF and GTC share a deep commitment to the restoration of prophetic ministry to the church. Students will gain a biblical perspective on this dimension of the Spirit's work as they grow in hearing God's present-tense voice.

(10) Character formation

Power and wisdom are only part of the essential ingredients to a fruitful ministry. Students are challenged to deeper levels of holiness, humility, and compassion through the Grace Training Center curriculum and the ministry values of MVF.

About Metro Vineyard's Master's Commission

The Master's Commission is a nine-month residential discipleship training programme for men and women between the ages of eighteen and twenty-four. It serves as a 'boot camp' of intense Christian life training combining solid biblical teaching, life-challenging curriculum, and practical experience. This programme is an opportunity for students to broaden the foundation of their lives by giving themselves to serving the body through a practical daily lifestyle and learning about the lordship of Jesus. During this training time the student will experience many ministry opportunities with training concentrating on:

- Servanthood
- Character building
- Studying and applying the Bible
- Ministry of the Word
- Worship and intercession
- Evangelism and outreach

For more information about the Master's Commission, please fill out the form on page 252 and send it to us.

About Metro Vineyard Conferences

Metro Vineyard Fellowship periodically hosts conferences in Kansas City for training, equipping and encouraging the body of Christ at large. Joining Mike Bickle and the Metro Vineyard

Fellowship leadership team are leaders from around the nation. If you would like to receive information about future conferences hosted by Metro Vineyard Fellowship, please fill out the form on page 252 and send it to us.

Appendix IV

Mike Bickle's teaching tapes, books, conferences

You've probably just finished reading this book by Mike Bickle and may be wondering how you can get other resource materials by Mike. Well, we want to give you a gift by sending you a copy of his *Personal Prayer List*. Through this book he offers practical suggestions for turning Scripture to prayer and offering it back to the Lord as a powerful tool for advancing the kingdom. Mike's years of experience in the prayer closet make this a valuable tool for helping you develop your own devotional prayer life. Just photocopy, fill out the form, and mail it back to us! We'll send you a copy of his *Personal Prayer List* along with a coupon for 35% discount off your next tape order from our catalogue of Mike's ministry resources. Quantities of this booklet are limited and will be processed on a first-come, first-served basis.

Tapes by Mike Bickle

Ravished Heart of God (Vols 1 & 2)

The six tapes of Volume 1 and five tapes of Volume 2 are the course material from this unique series, taken from a Grace Training Center class. Perhaps no other book has so gripped

Mike Bickle in the last four years as the Song of Songs. Explored as an allegory of the relationship between the Lord Jesus and his church, Mike's teaching on this fascinating book is an inspiration. It's the faith-building, life-giving story of the Lord's heart, passionate for his bride, the church, to come forth in her glory as his companion and co-labourer.

Volume 1 A6RHG	$29.00
Volume 2 A5RHG2	$24.50
Study Notes	$8.00

Passion for the Lord Jesus

This seven-tape series allows Mike to pour out his heart in what has become widely identified as his 'life message'. Going beyond Mike's popular book, these tapes allow you to hear with your own ears the energy and passion in Mike's voice as he shares his heart's cry. These tapes will challenge the way you view and experience the Christian life.

A7PLJ $33.50

Kiss the Son

In this two-tape series on Psalm 2, Mike contrasts world events with eternal truths. Originally preached at Westminster Chapel in London, this message offers much-needed perspective in an increasingly troubled world. You'll be encouraged as you're reminded of God's omniscient wisdom and his eternal plan, coming together in these dangerous last days. Faith building.

A2KTS $10.50

Overcoming Spiritual Mid-Life Crisis

Did you know it's possible to have a spiritual mid-life crisis? There comes a time when every believer moves beyond youthful enthusiasm; a time when one begins to process the hopes and disappointments of life in the kingdom. Mike will help guide you through this tumultuous season with honesty,

humour and candour in a three-tape series.
A30SM $15.00

The Passions of God's Personality

The apostle Paul joyfully embraced a life of radical obedience
and costly hardship. Why? How? He identifies his secret in
Philippians 3:8 as 'the surpassing greatness of the deep knowledge of Christ Jesus'. The driving force in Paul's life was the
magnetic appeal of the beauty and splendour of who God is. In
this Grace Training Center seminar, Mike probes the depths of
God's personality as the key to a life of holy abandonment and
glad-hearted sacrifice. Two tapes.
A2PGP $10.50

When Anointed Leaders Fall

Few experiences in the Christian life can bring such disillusionment so quickly. These tapes will help you through the valley
and get you back up the other side. Sincere, filled with grace
and mercy, these tapes will help every believer.
A3WAL $15.00

Lessons in the Prophetic

In this two-tape series, Mike Bickle offers some candid, honest,
real-life insights into the prophetic. Gleaned from ten years'
involvement with some of the most celebrated prophetic ministries in the world, Mike offers a less-than-glamorous look at
prophetic realities, strengths and dangers.
A2LINP $10.50

A Song of Love

This two-tape series takes a detailed look at Psalm 45. Mike
explores this extraordinary song of love with insight and reve
lation. As always, Mike's teaching is solidly biblical and
refreshing in its simplicity. These tapes will stir in you a deeper

love for Jesus.
A2SOL $10.50

Overview of the Song of Solomon

If you don't have the time or the interest to work through Mike's Training Center class on the Song of Solomon through the two-volume set above, this two-tape overview is for you.
A2OSS $10.50

To order tapes and to receive a free catalogue of books and tapes by Mike Bickle, Paul Cain, John Wimber and many others, call 001-816-763-3070 or (USA only) 1-800-552-2449.

Photocopy and mail to Grace Ministries, PO Box 229, Grand-view, MO 64030-0229, USA.

Name ....
Address...
....
Church you attend ....
Church address ....
....

❏ Please send information about The Master's Commission.
❏ Please send information about Metro Vineyard Conferences with Mike Bickle.
❏ Please send information about Grace Training Center of Kansas City.
❏ Please send a resource catalogue of Mick Bickle's ministry resources.

Passion for Jesus

by Mike Bickle

Perfecting extravagant love for God.

Do you know how God feels about you?
How you answer that question will determine the
nature of your spiritual life.

As a young man, Mike Bickle was consumed with zeal
for the gospel. Taught by his father to train hard and
go for broke, it was no surprise that when Mike became
a Christian, his commitment was total. He memorised
whole chapters of the Bible; he prayed for hours; he
fasted; he 'witnessed' fervently to others about his
faith.

The ingredients for an angry, self-righteous Pharisee
were in place.

Passion for Jesus tells how the grace of God set Mike free
and led him into the birthright of every believer – a
knowledge of God's overpowering and intimate love.

'Anyone who knows Mike Bickle knows that he has
subordinated everything in his life to this one goal:
acquiring a passion for Jesus. And therein lies the
power of this book.'

– JACK DEERE
Author of *Surprised by the Power of the Spirit*

 Kingsway Publications